My
Unrelenting Darkness
An autobiographical recounting

by

Thomas D. Atherton

MY UNRELENTING DARKNESS
An autobiographical accounting
By Thomas David Atherton
is an original publication of *The Family of Man Press*.

The Family of Man Press
A division of G. F. Hutchison Press
319 South Block Avenue, Suite 17
Fayetteville, AR 72701

Copyright © 2007, by Gary F Hutchison
ISBN: 0-9796279-2-3
    978-0-9796279-2-7

Printed in USA

PR 10 9 8 7 6 5 4 3 2

Dedication

To Carole,
without whom, in my latter stages of recovery, my struggle
would have been so much lonelier, difficult, and prolonged –
perhaps impossible.
To John,
whose presence in my life these past few years,
has provided my reason to keep to the struggle.
To my family
who believed I would return, and when I did, stood ready with
open arms and open hearts.
Especially to my father
whose wonderful smile and gentle hug proved to me beyond
any doubt that I was finally back where I belonged.
And finally
to that unrelenting darkness, itself,
which allowed me to revisit the stuff from which – underneath
it all – I and all human beings are made: love, compassion,
caring, helpfulness, determination to survive, and a belief in
the absolute preciousness of mankind.

T.D.A. July 25, 2007

Table of Contents

Preface

This morning I went from my living room into my kitchen to get something. Arriving in the kitchen I drew a complete blank about what I had come for. I smiled. I probably even chuckled because I knew I could go back through that portal – the doorway – and chances were it would all pop back into mind. Unlike many 'mature' folks, for reasons that will soon become clear, I eagerly embrace such moments.

I have just emerged from nineteen years on the blank side of life's portal with no idea how to locate it and pass back through it to find my answers. During that time my previous life was blacked out as if erased by some malevolent, memory-sucking, magnet.

This is that story but it is also much more. It is an exploration of the deepest part of the human mind and how it works tirelessly to protect us and our sanity. It is a tribute to human ingenuity, resilience, strength, and determination. It is a cautionary note about the tenuousness of reality. In the end it is a story of love. Its page-by-page essence, however, portrays my terrifying struggle to fight my way back out of My Unrelenting Darkness.

Names of people and places have been modified to protect the individuals involved from those who would irresponsibly pry and from those with malicious intent.

CHAPTER ONE:
My terror is never ending!

There it is again. The phone. Three calls since I turned in for the night. Three excruciatingly long moments of silence when I answered. No breathing. No background sounds. Just empty silence. Each time I hope for a dial tone. What a dismal state it is when your greatest comfort in life is to be met by the sterile, monotonous, drone of a dial tone.

Should I pick up? If I don't, it will just ring on into the night. It has happened before. It could be kids pranking and I could just be a random victim. It could be my unseen nemesis drawing the noose just a bit tighter in his continuing, relentless, quest to drive me over the edge. I will detach the phone from the line. That done, I will obsess, of course, wondering if the caller is still on the line. I will worry – worry if *that* might have been the time there would have been some message – a message of hope, a message of my imminent demise, either – any – just *some* message.

There is a car parked across the street – unhidden, boldly, blatantly, sitting beneath the light. I can see it through the peep hole in my door. It has been there other nights. Are its occupants waiting for me? Are they watching? Are they part of this conspiracy to suck sanity from my being? Is their intent to wait until they believe I am asleep and come and do harm to me? That is my belief. It is why my lights burn all night, every night. Are these fears and assessments reasonable or paranoid? They have guided my life all these years. Perhaps my very existence verifies their truth.

How many years has this been going on – fifteen, eighteen, more? It is not how my life was supposed to go. This hiding and moving and making sure I leave no trail is not living. It is surviving moment by moment in terror. Why is it that I cannot come by so much as a speck of reliable, solid, information about why, how, it all came about? Am I a bad guy with the authorities closing in? Am I a good guy with some evil person or organization seeking to do me in? If I only knew I could at long last begin working toward some real solution.

I will eventually fall asleep tonight. I always do. The Fright with which I coexist has long been my one certainty – the single dependable feature of my life. Oddly, if it were to leave me I would have nothing. The likelihood of its departure is not really a concern. Worry will not banish it. Logic cannot conquer it. Surrender is not my style. Tonight, like every night, we lay here side by side, my Fright and I. The same two, well worn, questions will linger in my mind as I close my consciousness for the day: Who am I, and how – why – have I been doomed to endure this terrifying existence?

A story should start at the beginning but for the past nineteen years there has been no beginning. I have had no anchor in time or place or identity. I have had no timeline that carried me from youth into the present.

I am confident that I can share with the reader in great detail the exact progression of the story as it unfolded. I am less confident that I can as effectively convey the soul depleting, horrific, emotional side of the experience. However, I will give that my best effort because in truth, *that* is the story. We skip back in time.

* * * * *

At 11:36 on the morning of August 20, 1990 I suddenly discovered myself on a back street in downtown Joplin. It was as if I had emerged from a mist of nothingness. In fact, I remember glancing back as if expecting to see it. I was carrying a well-scarred suitcase in my right hand and had a

10

khaki, canvas, duffle bag slung over my left shoulder. I had no idea who I was, where I was, where I had come from, or why I was there.

A paralyzing wave of panic – no terror – washed over me. I initiated a quick check. I knew the date. I knew who the president was. I knew my age – fifty-two. At least I was pretty sure that was my age. I couldn't recall my birth date – something / something / 1938. I didn't know why I so quickly began asking myself those particular questions.

I let that go and moved to a park bench under a tree in a small, planted, area behind *The Something National Bank*. The heat reflecting from the pavement boiled up in sweltering waves and I welcomed even the modest relief offered by the shade and the coolness of the, dew moist, green, grassy, carpet. I felt for my wallet. It was in my rear left pocket. I removed it and examined the contents. There were lots of one hundred dollar bills. I didn't stop to count them. There was no driver's license or other ID. There were two pictures of young, teen-age, boys. I didn't recognize them but felt I should. Nothing else save a deeply creased outline divulging the once upon a time whereabouts of a key – obviously important in my past life. All quite briefly I was able to appreciate the humor it presented – even *that* safety net was gone.

I found myself breathing way too rapidly. I dared not hyperventilate, faint, and become the focus of local attention – not until I had things sorted out. I made a conscious effort to regain control. I closed my eyes. Oddly, I thought, the image of a black apple came into focus. It self-generated the phrase, "Relax and focus." As if from a wish granted by a benevolent genie those two things were immediately set in place. I relaxed. The movement of my chest returned to normal. After a few moments I opened my eyes and got back to work, setting aside my puzzlement for another time. I took hope that the rest of my unsettling situation would be dispatched with similar ease.

I needed a plan but became preoccupied with details. I was wearing dark blue dress slacks – too heavy for summer – with a belt and cuffs and buttoned rear pockets. My shirt was short sleeved, light blue, button down the front, a pen and comb in the left pocket. I needed a shower. I would not have been described as slender. In the right front pants pocket were several coins; in the left was a large, oddly shaped, flat, metal, key. I turned it over. Greyhound #104. A storage box at a bus station. Was I headed to a bus or had I recently disembarked from one? How did I even know about bus station lock boxes? Again, who was I? Where had I come from? Where was I headed? Why? How? My questions became one with my initial terror.

I was taken by the quality of the vocabulary that presented itself in my thoughts. It produced a short-lived smile, the first I'd known – ever known, it seemed. Back to the plan. The tattered half of a manila check tag was tied to the suitcase handle – it confirmed the 'Greyhound connection'. I placed the suitcase on my lap. Before opening it I surveyed the area with the shifty-eyed caution of a spy in a smoke filled cabaret out of a 1940's, black and white, 'B' movie. There were stubs from tickets documenting a ride from Kansas City to Joplin dated the day before. There must have been things left at the station in the lock box – things that I couldn't manage or didn't feel safe carrying. I would find a place to stay – a motel or such – and then search out the bus depot. Such as it was, *that* became my plan.

A very short, very old, lady with her very large, very young Black Lab approached and took a seat nearby. I needed information on several fronts so engaged her in small talk. She was pleased to chat but tended to ramble well beyond the short, concise, answers I desired. An agitated Rover – Lord Mountbatten the Fourth, to be perfectly accurate – was clearly not certain as to the propriety of the interchange. The city was indeed Joplin. The bus station was four blocks north, the direction from which I had come. There was a classy hotel several blocks away on the main drag to the east and a run down motel three to the west. I thanked her and headed west feeling the need to conserve everything – money, energy, mental effort. Either I was not a dog person or the 'Lord' was not empathetic to lost souls. I believe that we were each relieved at the parting.

My anxiety grew as I walked. The intensity of my suspicion about those I passed amazed me. It was clearly an unfamiliar – uncharacteristic – reaction or way of life for me. I took some solace in that fact but wondered how it could really be, considering it came so easily. Regardless, at that moment, it was anxiety, suspicion, and great fear – all unattached to anything within my grasp – that characterized my reality.

I located the motel and found the manager inside the first, open, door. Her disordered kitchen table served as the front desk.

"Ten bucks a day or fifty a week," she announced. "By the week I need to see ID. Don't need none by the day."

"I guess I'll have to go with daily, then. I was mugged yesterday in Kansas City and it was ID and credit cards they were after."

She – *Candy,* as it turned out – was pushing seventy, generally unkempt, with a cigarette dangling from the corner of her garishly, bright, red, lips. She held her unbuttoned, dark blue, robe closed at her bosom.

"Three nights?"

Unintentionally, it had spilled from my mouth as if it were a question.

She took my money without responding. Apparently receipts were not part of the arrangement. At the outset she had appeared almost compassionate about my misfortune up in KC. Seeing the rows of bills standing crisp in my wallet, her eyebrow raised. She didn't refer to it. I wondered where my instant 'robbery' explanation had come from. True? Fabrication? I didn't know. I did know that I had no ID or credit cards. I also quickly came to understand that I had to become far more cautious in my dealings with people. I was trusting. At the outset, at least, that seemed like an inappropriate approach to this world in which I found myself – the one in which I suddenly had to learn to cope and survive. Care, suspicion, distance – those things had come to necessarily redefine my every move, every thought, every plan.

The low, flat roofed, 1940's, structure was finished in

13

stucco, its once white paint yellowed with age and patterned with spreading, long unattended, rusty red, cracks. The roof was tar over tarpaper over ancient shingles, their still red mineral surface peaking through here and there, randomly redirecting tiny bursts of sunshine. The soffit above the door to room 13 – the only free standing room – hung loose. A mouse appeared in the opening and gave me the once over. I must have passed muster as it flicked its whickers, turned, and left back into the dark filth of the innards of the ancient building. I sensed a kinship.

Inside my room, behind locked door, my first act was to search my bags for clues. There was nothing remotely helpful. Well, there were clothes, yellow pads, and two socks cram packed with more hundred dollar bills.

With that and the two thousand plus in my wallet, I felt well healed and, for the time being, relaxed a bit. Other things became more important than counting it. The room was small, its dusty, dark, paneling riddled with nail holes. It was musty smelling – much like myself.

I showered and changed, leaving most things as they were in my bags in case I might need to move on quickly. I didn't know the source of that feeling, but it was as close to a memory as I had so I went with it.

The plain looking man in the mirror was a stranger – white hair, round face, clear skin, average teeth, blue eyes, regular nose, bushy eyebrows. I thought that perhaps I should grow a beard in order to change my appearance. There was a twelve inch, long-healed, scar running diagonally down the right side of my plumpish, hairy, abdomen – gall bladder, I assumed.

I needed to eat and to go in search of the lockbox at the bus station. In that short, half hour, the room had become my sanctuary – my fortress – the only familiar aspect in my life. The thought of leaving it was discomforting – more than that it was cause for painful, gut wrenching, anxiety. I looked out the north window and then peeked through the permanently closed mini-blind covering the small, peek-a-boo, pane on the door. There was no activity – well, there was the spider hard at work securing the still struggling moth into its web at the

14

window – but no one in sight outside. Somehow I felt a strong and immediate connection with the moth. I had no idea what I was expecting to find out there or how I would determine its safe or treacherous features. Eventually, I mustered my courage and left.

With both tasks soon accomplished – chicken fried steak with all the trimmings and the trip to the depot – I was back in my place of safety within the hour. It was nearing two o'clock. The lockbox at the bus station had been at floor level and the largest available. It held a single piece of luggage – a king sized, soft sided, suitcase on rollers and was heavy, bulged to its limits. It appeared to be brand new.

Inside it was a computer with a small screen monitor. There was also an unopened box of floppy disks, a radio/tape player, and a small TV. They were packed in blankets and sheets. There were other odds and ends as well. I recognized none of it but smiled at the title on the yellow and black book – *Computers for Dummies*. It looked unused. Perhaps I remembered about it. Perhaps not.

I was disappointed at my unenlightening find. I was tired so lay down to rest. My inclination was to remove my shoes. My uncertainty required that they be left on. I awoke at a little after five not really refreshed. The bed was not bad. I was disappointed that things had not cleared up for me – my past life, identity, the reason for my presence there in Joplin. I would have settled for my name. My, how I would have settled for my name!

The terror returned as alternating ripples of hot and cold clawing their ways through my body just under my skin. In desperation, I hit the side of my head with the ball of one hand as if that might jar the appropriate memories to the foreground of my mind. It didn't. Not even the second or third or fourth or fifth blow delivered anything of use. My temple was bruised. How dumb. Perhaps that yellow book had, in fact, been written with me in mind.

My thoughts became scattered. Café dining was going to be too expensive. I needed to find a grocery. There was a hotplate, sink, and tiny fridge – an aluminum combination unit – under the rear window. I opened the refrigerator. It was cold. There was one small tray of ice cubes – hard. The small space would handle a half gallon of milk and a few other items. I dumped the cubes and flushed the tray under gallons of fresh water. I had once read – or perhaps written – a short story in which poison had been delivered via ice cubes. I filled and replaced the tray. When turned on high, the electric hotplate glowed red. The water flowed with some force from the faucet and exited in a lazy eddy through the small drain hole at the bottom of the black stained sink.

The back window housed the air conditioner – old, unquiet, and without a front panel. It did a reasonable job at cooling the place. After ten minutes spent with a toothpick cleaning its dust infused front louvers, it actually worked very well. It sounded happier, I thought.

The room was twelve feet square with a low ceiling and a squeaky, more or less carpeted, wooden, floor. The door had both a button lock in the knob and a separate dead bolt. One key worked both. There was a small, black and white TV suspended from a black, tubular, frame in the corner to the left of the door. The bed was opposite it between the front wall and the bathroom door. A tiny wooden table and two chairs sat beyond, between that door and the sink in the rear. A recliner – clearly the most recent addition – sat in the opposite rear corner with a direct view of the TV up front. Under the north window was a dresser, its rear right leg replaced – apparently with permanent intent – by two, carelessly stacked, Gideon Bibles.

It would be my home for who knew how long. At seventy dollars a week – fifty if I could work out the ID problem or charm Candy into allowing it – the place seemed a bargain. Candy seemed uncharmable so in my plan I'd settle on seventy.

I felt like a nothing, a nobody, a lost little lamb. Lambs were kindly images. It made me wonder if I even fit *that* category. Most likely I was on the run, hence the initial reluctance to really unpack or remove my shoes, and the anxiety I experienced at leaving the room and later when I spotted a policeman. I seemed to be carrying all my possessions with me. I wanted to scream. I didn't. That wouldn't help.   Quite clearly that was not my style. Apparently I was a well disciplined sort. Nevertheless, I didn't know how much longer I could take it, and 'it' was scarcely six hours old! Perhaps after a complete night's sleep things would begin falling into place.

I was drawn again to the photos in my wallet. The boys pictured there were fourteen – maybe fifteen. One was in color – faded – and the other black and white – dog-eared and scarred. I knew the faces yet I didn't. They were familiar to the extent that as my eyes met theirs I was filled with warmth of a kind. Perhaps they would be my link. I removed them from the yellowed, plastic, photo holder and laid them on the table.

My attention returned to the contents of the large suitcase I had retrieved from the bus station. What could I learn about me?   Upon inspection I found that the little computer was new. The white, slick covered, Tandy, manual had not yet been bent back to provide access to its helpfulness. The several cables were still factory secured with those ubiquitous, black, plastic, ties. The ten inch, used, TV was color showing twenty some channels on its dial. There were rabbit ears. It had all been carefully packed using two single bed sheets, a blue, wool blanket, two pillow cases, four blue towels, and a tan and red uniform shirt bearing the Dairy Queen logo. Hmm? Did all that suggest that I watched TV and slept a lot, being too lazy to look into actually using the new computer?? I hoped that initial characterization would prove to be faulty at several points.

A number of things were clear. I hadn't clue-one about how to operate a computer. I had no memories of a Dairy Queen. The logo shirt was well worn and wrinkled. Perhaps it was a rag I had acquired for cleaning. Perhaps not. Oddly the floppy disks came in two sizes. The sample taken from the cellophane wrapped box – about three inches by three and three quarters – fit into the slit on the computer. The half dozen held together as a set by wide, rubber bands, did not. They were smaller and thicker. Later I would seek assistance at a Radio Shack or some such place and sort that out. How did I remember about Radio Shack and not about myself?

17

I felt the distinct need to walk the streets and become acquainted with downtown Joplin and the surrounding area. That was a task for broad daylight, not waning twilight. The café I had found was on a side street, eight blocks from the motel and one from the main north-south thoroughfare. I hadn't got its name but did spy another restaurant across the busy street to the east. The Post Office was on the next corner north, directly across from the library and kitty-cornered from the bank, behind which I had taken refuge that first morning. I had a few landmarks but nothing more. I'm sure Candy would point me toward a grocery in the morning.

I fluffed a pillow and set it against the bed's head board. I lay back, having removed my shoes that time. I had to get a handle on *something*. Okay. I was in Joplin in August, a man in his early fifties with no ID, sufficient money for a while, and not so much as a clue to as to what saleable skills he might possess in case earning a living became a necessity. I had been pretty good innovating with that toothpick earlier. Maybe a handyman. My blue dress slacks and nice shirts suggested otherwise. Otherwise *what*, I had no idea.

I needed to begin a list so extracted a yellow pad from the smaller suitcase. I used the pen from my shirt pocket.

1- find a grocery store within walking distance

2- go to the library and roam the stacks to find clues to my profession.

3- learn about establishing an identity solid enough to survive on (on which to survive). Interesting! Perhaps there had been an education in my past. Number three might necessitate a trip to a book store.

4- devise a way to hide and protect my money.

5- devise a way to hide and protect myself.

Those five things came to mind in rapid fire succession. I would add others as they presented themselves. I laid the pad beside me on the bed and surveyed the room. My anxiety had lessened from overwhelming to merely extremely discomforting. A third smile. If anything, however, my suspiciousness had grown and suddenly became the mainstay of my personality. Protect old _____ at any cost. Protect who? George? Harry? Clarence? David? Peter? Sam? I had no name. When needing one to sign the register earlier I had written Jim Johnson, pulling it, on the spot, out of thin air – at least I had to assume that. Candy hadn't questioned it. I imagine she has known many Jim Johnsons, Sam Smiths, and John Jones. The place would be a magnet for that ilk – apparently *my* ilk. I decided that I would refer to myself by name, only when absolutely necessary and then I would continue to use just Jim – Jim Johnson *only* when pressed. Clearly, obtaining a name and some proof of it had to be high in my priorities.

Thoughts careened in and out of my head. That pleased me. I hoped to capture some that held promise of answers. One such thought took me back to the fully unexpected, black apple image I had experienced earlier on the park bench. I seemed to know about such things. It was a well practiced mental marker that allowed immediate access to relaxation as was a prerequisite to self-hypnosis and pain management. How did I know that? My black apple had been deliberately set in place earlier, just waiting to be utilized. Hypnosis. Relaxation techniques. I took note. Surely those things would be important in defining who I was – probably something quite different from a toothpick wielding handyman. Perhaps, nothing more than a well therapied, mental patient. Had I escaped from an institution of some sort?

At that point my state could not be referred to as relaxed although the situation was becoming less frantic, less terrifying, than it had been. That is, it had been the case up until *that* particular moment.

Suddenly I saw the red, swirling, lights of a police car just outside my room. Obviously it had been a silent approach. How did I know about such a thing? I put on my shoes and laced them tight. It was as if by reflex. Panic welled up within me. I moved to the door and carefully raised one blind slat just high enough so I could peek out. It was dusk – light enough to make out figures but not enough to see them distinctly.

Candy and the policeman were speaking in the middle of the long, narrow parking lot. They looked one way and then the other. They each pointed from time to time – never

19

actually in the direction of my room. The officer waved her away and drew his weapon. My heart sank. He moved south across the lot – south was my direction. As he came close to the building I lost sight of him. I went to the north window and flattened myself against the wall, peeking out just enough to get him in view. He kept close to the front wall and continued moving south. He passed the open space between me and the main building to the north. There was a final section of the motel on the south side of my room. It housed rooms 14, 15, and 16.

I saw the policeman's shadow cross the window in my front door. There was a small window in the bathroom but it contained frosted glass and was high up next to the ceiling. I took a kitchen chair with me and stood on it, opening that window just a crack – it easily swung toward me once the sliding lock was disengaged. I was just in time to see the figure move past my room and on down the line.

There was a loud thumping on a door as the officer announced himself. It should have been good news – he was not after me. Suspicion reigned in my head, however. Perhaps he had the wrong room. Perhaps Candy had misled him on my behalf. I returned to the main room and again looked north out the side window. I fully expected to see her standing there motioning me to leave and follow her to safety. She was not there. My fantasy came to a swift, reason induced, halt. I had to keep my mind under better control.

I had broken into a swift, soaking, sweat. So much for the value of my shower. I waited at the front door peering out through the window. Presently the officer returned with a scruffy looking, bare-chested, bare footed, young man in handcuffs. I was so relieved – for me. I felt a wave of compassion for the youngster. It drew me back to the pictures on the table. I had no idea why. I found myself crying.

What began as a few wayward trickles down my cheeks as I reached out and touched the faces pictured there, soon escalated into a pillow drenching down pour. I buried my face in the bed and sobbed on convulsively for many minutes. How long I could not be sure. I awakened at midnight. I rolled over onto my back my new reality rushing in on me.

20

My cheeks were still damp. I felt some better – me and my still blank mind felt some better. I checked the locks, undressed, turned off the lights, and returned to bed hoping for a more restful experience than my early day nap had provided.

Upon awakening the next morning I was immediately disappointed on several fronts. I didn't feel rested. No new pieces of my puzzle burst on the scene to provide the relief I hoped for. I was suddenly hit by the real possibility that this might be all I'd ever know about myself – my past. The sheer terror triggered by that realization, became overwhelming. In the process it seemed to stir the boiling cauldron of my subconscious and force new data to the surface.

There had been a dream that night. Its illusive remnant was dark and swirling and ominously oppressive. Contemplating it caused my stomach to churn and I came close to losing my supper. Interesting. I had failed to think about eating supper the night before. Perhaps that was the real reason for my gastric gyrations. No. It was more.

I comforted my head back into the pillow, closed my eyes, and called up the black apple. It was clearly a well practiced, habitual, behavior in times of stress. My body, which had been tensed taut by that first minute or so of my morning's mental activity, immediately relaxed. My breathing slowed. The image of the shiny, black, apple was encompassed by a soft, gently swirling, blue, fog – mist perhaps or translucent smoke. I told myself to return to the dream – to experience it in its totality. How did I know to do that?

It caused me to sleep. A few minutes later I awoke, sitting up straight in bed again terrified, my chest heaving as if I'd been chasing a fifteen year old uphill. I was immediately visited by my fourth smile. This was a *good* kind of terrified because it, unlike the others I had experienced, was tied to something I could remember. The dream or at least a dream. I would assume *the,* not merely *a*. It seemed so real that, without hesitation, I took it to heart as fact.

It had been a seemingly endless, horrendous, nightmare in which shadowy, thug-types (or maybe plain clothes police or federal agents) were chasing me down dark alleys, up fire

21

escapes, and across the roofs of tall buildings where I was forced to all quite recklessly and without hesitation, leap over open spaces ten stories above the street. I had to just keep running with no apparent objective other than to mindlessly elude my adversaries. The accompanying emotion was sheerest terror as if being herded into a blind canyon with no real expectation of ever surviving the ordeal.

The clear message was that somebody with malevolent intentions was after me – good guys or bad guys, however, I couldn't tell. Additionally, of course, if they were good, I was bad. If I was good, they were bad. My clear mission from that moment on was to keep myself hidden (and out of box canyons!). I fretted for a moment that there was but one door in my room. The bathroom window would serve to extricate me in a pinch.

It handled one question that had been popping in and out of my mind: Should I contact the local authorities to engage their help – have them check me out through their missing persons data base? *I should not*, at least not until I got a better handle on things. I didn't seem like a bad guy but I supposed if I could blank out a lifetime I could also blank that out. Why I would, remained a festering, though fascinating, question.

The new configuration of my situation clearly posed new barriers to finding my identity and answering the questions about why I had erased my mind of all that seemed truly important – family, occupation, personal history, name. Plainly, the usual means and help sources would not be available to me. I would have to proceed carefully, crafting and carrying out new and ingenious plans. That prospect momentarily lightened my burden. It was as if perhaps crafting and carrying out new and ingenious plans was a familiar and satisfying activity. Yea or nay, I hoped I was good at it.

It was as if I suddenly had a purpose and could move away from the nothingness that followed me as I emerged out onto the sidewalk some twenty hours earlier.

I was suddenly hungry. I showered and dressed and, addressing the world from each opening in my room, soon felt safe enough to exit and go after breakfast.

Candy was sweeping the sidewalk. I stopped to pass the time of day.

"Good morning, Candy. Looks like a pretty day."

She squinted and looked up into the sky shading her eyes with her hand.

"It'll be a scorcher by noon. No relief in the forecast. I hate summer. But then, I hate winter, too."

I doubted if more chipper talk from me would actually help brighten her day so I asked my question.

"Is there a grocery close by?"

She hitched her head to the west.

"IGA. Three blocks. Nice store. Offers money orders and such as well."

"Thanks. Thought I'd give that kitchen unit a tryout for lunch."

"A man who cooks. Now, that's a hoot!"

It wasn't the part of my conversation that I had intended to bring her a smile but from her lingering chuckles I had apparently hit her funny bone. One never knows. Yah! Tell me about it!!!

The café offered a good breakfast. My preferred fare jumped off the menu immediately: orange juice, pancakes, sausage patties, and black coffee – lots of black coffee. I figured that at least one of four was probably not harmful to my body. Another smile. Was that number four or five? Perhaps I had reached the point where I no longer needed to keep count. How nice.

I lingered there in what seemed to be the comfort and safety of the corner booth dressed, as it was, in the official dark red Naugahyde uniform of respectable corner booths everywhere. The older gentleman who ran the place offered friendly, if meaningless, chit chat each time he approached and refilled my cup. His name was Edgar – Edgar Bergen. He said he called his wife *Charlie – Mortimer* if he was upset with her. He enjoyed his little joke; one that would have whisked right over the head of a younger patron.

The grocery was large with wide varieties in quality and price. At first I just walked the aisles trying to establish my taste menu. Microwave dinners seemed most familiar. Fresh

23

fruit caught my eye as well. Soup. I was amazed at how many cans of soup there were. Five shelves high and some forty feet long. How would a dyslexic possibly cope when confronted with such an array? How did I know about dyslexics? Why would I be so immediately concerned?

I settled on a half dozen soups, a bag of oranges and apples, a half gallon of milk and one of OJ, a loaf of bread, some soft margarine, a variety pack of luncheon meat, and a pack of little, white, donuts. Veggies didn't seem to rank high in my preferences. As an afterthought I added a box of cheerios and a hundred watt light bulb.

I also picked up two small African Violet plants – pink and white, their pots wrapped in shiny, lilac, foil. I checked out, took a deep breath, and walked – hurried – the several blocks back to my oasis. I kept watch over my shoulder, several times spotting suspicious men only to have them turn off or walk in the other direction.

As I passed Candy's open door – why she didn't use her AC if she hated hot weather so I couldn't figure – I called hello. She came to the door, her new, freshly pressed, hot pink, robe fastened around her waist with a red, silk-look, scarf. Her hair was combed. Perhaps my first impression had been drawn from an off day.

"Found the store, I guess," She said leaning against the door frame and lighting a new cigarette from the barely glowing stub of it predecessor.

"Sure did. Right where you said it would be."

Could I have possibly opened with a more inane response?

Perhaps in reparation for that comment or just because I felt sorry for her, I took the pink blossomed plant from my bag and handed it over.

"For your kindnesses since I've been here," I said. I meant it.

I didn't wait for a response but moved on down the sidewalk to number 13. It was the first time I was struck by the number and all the ominous ramifications that it held for so many people. In choosing to ignore it I learned still another thing about myself. There had actually been two things if I

24

also chalked up the kindly act I had bestowed on the lonely lady up the walk. I hesitated briefly hoping to see my new friend – the mouse. He was apparently engaged elsewhere. Perhaps snuggling with his girl friend. I hoped so.

I locked the door and turned on the light – a clip-on-to-a-bulb type plastic fixture hugging the center of the ceiling. I began putting the groceries away. There was a knock on the door. Immediately my heart began thumping, visible on my chest. I approached the door and peeped through the pane.

It was Candy. I sighed, took several deep breaths, and opened it, greeting her.

"Hey! Candy. What can I do for you?"

She raised her eyebrows, leaned back, and looked me over in places I had not intended to insinuate by the remark.

"If you're gonna cook you need some pans and dishes and stuff. I put some together for ya. I expect them back when ya leave out."

She offered a bulging, plastic, grocery, bag.

"How kind and thoughtful of you. Thank you. You know, I had completely overlooked that part of the housekeeping thing."

"I got a spare broom. If ya want it, drop by."

She turned and started back toward her apartment. Apparently house cleaning was not included in the seventy a week deal.

I replaced the forty watt in the ceiling with the new hundred watt bulb. The room suddenly burst into brightness. The down side to that was being able to see the justification for the broom Candy had mentioned.

I tried setting the violet in several windows, finally settling on the north one where I could easily see it from both the bed and the recliner. I liked flowers. Did that make a sissy? I turned on the TV. Fourteen inches of fuzzy black and white images. *Eight channels* of fuzzy black and white images. Turning the little dials and punching the little buttons across the bottom of the set did not improve things. I spent the next fifteen minutes replacing it with the little color set I had brought with me. Mine was older and had no easy way of hooking into the cable so I figured out how to attach the rabbit ears and hung them from a nearby hook in the ceiling. I ran through the channels. The picture was small but clearer and . . . well . . . more colorful. I did seem to have a way of pointing out the obvious. In the end, I found I could receive three channels well and one that was marginal. Perhaps it would be better by night. Television really didn't seem to be an important part of my life.

I was learning interesting and useful things about myself. In general, I really liked what I was finding. Why was it, then, that somebody else didn't? Maybe this wasn't psychological Amnesia. I went into the bathroom and examined my head in front of the mirror, pulling my hair this way and that to bare my scalp and look for bruises. Perhaps I had fallen and hit my head causing physically induced, temporary, amnesia. I knew that sometimes happened. How did I know that? I found nothing except the spot on my temple on which I had so foolishly, repeatedly, clobbered myself the previous afternoon. I felt the entire surface to determine if there might me a tender area. There wasn't. I worked my way down the back of my neck. Nada! I re-combed my hair. Having combed hair seemed important to me.

I was clearly disappointed with my findings – my lack of findings, I suppose. Usually finding oneself in good shape was cause for joy. Not so.

I decided to continue working down the list I started the evening before. Establishing ID seemed to be the most immediate concern. I would venture forth to locate a bookstore and see what information I might find there. Then I would visit the library and walk the stacks in search of whatever presented itself as meaningful or relevant.

I mused. Perhaps there is no problem. Maybe babies aren't born or found under cabbage leaves. Maybe they tumble out of clouds of nothingness on the back streets of Joplin, Missouri. Perhaps, being directionally challenged, I got lost in the fog and it just took me longer to make my way into the world.

I had intended it to seem humorous. It didn't.

CHAPTER TWO:
Unsettling In!

The first bookstore was a grand place with front facing book displays, many arranged by author. There were comfortable chairs and lamps and tables for those who cared to linger. It was a classier store than I needed but I enjoyed walking the aisles in search of something familiar. None of the recent offerings struck a chord although memories of good friends from the classics offered comfortable feelings. With some reluctance I left, telling myself I would return and enjoy the ambiance if not a good book. It seemed obvious that reading the best sellers had not been my thing in recent years — unless that had fled from me along with other things.

I left with some reluctance, partly because of my apparent love of books and partly due to my general reluctance to expose myself out in the open. (Perhaps there might be a better way to phrase that!) I sucked it up, checked my zipper, and left, walking the ten blocks to the next store.

The fleshy, Playboy, poster in its window gave me some hope it might hold what I needed – that is, a lower brow book about underground survival – about moving through life in the shadows. I must say the image from the window did not easily fade. I was amazed at just how much three roses could cover. It required a second glance.

It was a corner building, small and cluttered with

columns of floor to ceiling shelves. There were stacks of magazines here and boxes of books there. I was somewhat amused that clutter did not bother me. In some ways it even felt comforting. The proprietor – early sixties, wire rim half lenses, receding, long, graying hair tied into a pony tail – busied himself near the register and gave no indication he had seen me enter, although he had. Perhaps anonymity was promised there. There were no signs to indicate genre – I had to wonder if the term, *genre*, had ever been uttered within those walls – so I began my search at one end and would work my way across the store.

Presently, I came upon the section for which I was searching. Guerilla this and guerilla that seemed to be the hallmark of the offerings. "How to Earn $50,000 a Year While Avoiding the IRS", "Living Underground for the Rest of Your Life", and finally, "How to Obtain Safe and Secure ID." I picked it up and looked at the table of contents. If it produced as promised, I had found what I needed. I also picked up a relatively thick paperback promising a thousand ways to make a living without leaving a financial paper trail. I hoped the obviousness of my choices would not raise suspicion with the old hippy at the register. Of course they would but clearly it would be of no real concern to him. It is why they were in the store – to be purchased. The two books came to $12.33. It seemed a bargain if they would actually come though for me.

I paused just outside – startling as the door clicked shut behind me. I searched the area with my eyes. How was I to possibly know if any of those present harbored evil intentions toward me? I moved west along the narrow street passing a dollar store. The ball cap displayed in the window caught my eye. Perhaps it would work to change my appearance. I entered and purchased one – dark blue, nondescript, largest size. My, I had a big head. A big *empty* head as it turned out. I also bought a quality, narrow, brief case – one with tumbler locks at the catches. I had a very specific plan for it.

Earlier, I had spotted an electronics store on the main drag. I headed for it. Inside I produced the half dozen smaller, thicker disks and asked the clerk if he knew about such things.

"They really aren't floppies," he began in a somewhat patronizing tone. "They're memory cards that go to a word processor. I think these are from a model sold at Sears or Penneys. To get more you'll have to go there. I'd suggest you move up to a computer, though. Word processors are becoming extinct just about as fast as they came on the scene. With your stuff on a floppy you can take it and read it anywhere."

I thanked him and said I would certainly consider his advice. It appeared that I had already made that decision either based on somebody else's advice or my own assessment of recent technology trends. I wondered how I might get a peek at what was on them. THAT intrigued me – captivated me – because certainly they must contain links to my past. I was suddenly excited. *Excited*, I discovered, was far better than *afraid*, although each seemed to produce similar rushes of adrenaline. Fascinating! It was not the specific physiological juices that characterized an emotion but one's characterization of that which initiated the flow. I knew that.

I shook off the psychological musings and returned my head to the present. I dared not let the suddenly preferable state of excitement lull me into acting carelessly or letting my guard down. It seemed obvious that precise mental book-keeping was going to be a crucial part of my life.

My next stop was the Library. It was a beautiful building that went far beyond the merely functional. It was in transition between card files and computer records. I was less interested in any of that than I was in topics, so I bypassed the area and moved directly into the stacks. I located the nonfiction area. I observed that the books were in need of attention by an anally compulsive neat freak. I chuckled out loud at how that phrase so comfortably combined a mixture of classic and popular psychobabble. How did I know that? As I recall I even smiled as I got to work. I began at archeology and moved on one shelf at a time past architecture and eventually biology. Soon into the task I noted that my glasses needed cleaning. They were bifocals. I hadn't noticed that before even though I had obviously been using them properly.

Although I had lingered with great interest over archeology, it was psychology – two thirds of the way through the alphabet – that really caught my eye. It was intriguing to realize the difference between interest and expertise. I pulled book after book off the shelves. Freud, Watson, James, Fromm, Skinner, even Snygg and Combes presented familiar venues. Reading the first sentence in a paragraph I could pretty well finish it on my own. I suddenly understood about the black apple and the connection to hypnosis that I had established in my mind. It amounted to a post hypnotic suggestion for relaxation and mental focus. It sent me back to more carefully consider the books dealing with hypnosis – specifically self-hypnosis. Perhaps it would be one of the keys or one of the methods to use as I searched for the keys.

Several new and ill-defined images flashed in my head. Me standing in front of a class of students – clearly college students. I looked so young. It faded and any details that may have been present vanished. I saw myself in a small room – a den or tiny living room or perhaps a professional office. It, too, vanished in a flash, but the picture of a child sitting on a couch lingered as an indistinct though powerful image – a memory, perhaps?? Had I just experienced my first two, true, memories, or were they merely the composition of a subconscious mind rushing in to satisfy my wishes? My! I seemed to indeed have some psychological expertise. Excitement – exuberance – exhilaration – all blossomed within me.

It was an interesting realization – revolution, I suppose – in the way I began thinking from that moment on. Rather than dismissing my apparent knowledge with, "How did I know that?" – which I realized translated as, "I probably really *don't* know that," – I began believing in what I knew. I paged through two books on hypnosis. I could have written them. It was cause for excitement – giddiness, even. I just needed time to let it all fall back into place. Interesting that although I had lost so much of my past I had not lost the academic side of the ledger. My immediate hope was that at least some personal memories would be so firmly attached to that knowledge that they would piggyback themselves into my consciousness.

30

Then, perhaps, I could begin to remembering about me as a person – as a personality – as a person with a name.

Something else. My amnesia might not be tied to my profession – I had not blocked out my knowledge – but about some other aspect of my life. I didn't know where to go with that or even if it might be important or useful so let it drop. It suggested intriguing possibilities, however.

I was immediately hit by the realization that I would not be able to use that professional knowledge to support myself. I had no credentials, no transcripts, no references, not even a name to use in looking myself up in the membership rolls of professional associations. Oddly, it brought me the broadest grin of those past several days. There I was, most likely sporting a PhD, with absolutely no saleable skills. I laughed out loud. What was that saying about "Piled Higher and Deeper?" Soon, however, I discovered the dampness covering my cheeks.

I dried my face and left the library, submitting to the requisite search of my briefcase at the front door. It angered me. Not the search. I understood about that. I was angry about a World in which there were people whose values allowed them – encouraged them – to steal and take advantage of the rest of us. It was a lazy mentality fully devoid of empathy and compassion and love for mankind as a species, and without that how could there be love of oneself?

By the time I got 'home' I realized that characterizing my earlier reaction as anger had been inappropriate. It was sadness taken to the nth power. My first inclination was to fix the problem, not punish the wrong doers. I had learned another important thing about myself. I wasn't a blamer. I was a fixer. I liked that. I liked that very much.

Even though I couldn't officially practice my psychological skills, I could still use them for the benefit of those around me – *and myself*. Perhaps I had already begun with Candy. In fact, giving of them freely seemed more legitimate than taking money for them, the way I supposed I had done in the past. That flash of the boy on the couch had been a young patient, I imagined. I wondered how much his parents had paid me to do whatever it was that I did for him.

In a sudden wave of sadness I hoped he was doing well – that my departure had not in any way harmed him. My reaction to that thought was simply overwhelming. Again I buried my face in the pillow and cried away the emotion. The reaction seemed light years out of proportion to that rather straight forward set of thoughts.

It was nearly noon when I awoke, drained and sad and generally discouraged. My morning had sent me to the highest highs and the lowest lows I had yet experienced. Such swings were not typical of me; I felt positive of that from toenails to follicles. I was a controlled, deliberate, mindful sort of man. I was not used to shedding tears for myself. I would try to learn from my reactions, examining them for their merits and putting them into proper perspective.

My early morning bowl of tiny O's had run its course and I was hungry. Deciding what to fix for lunch took my mind off the other things. Soup and sandwich with a glass of milk sounded good. Which soup? Cream of mushroom. I hesitated, considering the pros and cons of diluting it with water vs. milk. I went with the more expensive milk telling myself it would be more nutritious even though I recognized it was really because I liked it better that way. What kind of sandwich? Meat or peanut butter? I went with meat not knowing how well my little refrigerator would actually keep things fresh.

I heated the soup in Candy's pan. I poured the milk into Candy's glass. I set the table with Candy's plate and silverware. Thank you Candy for your kindness.

As I ate I fiddled with the radio trying to find an Oldie but Goody station that actually played songs ancient enough that I recognized them. Jolla! There it was. I ate slowly. The fare at . . . *Jim's* . . . table was not bad. I didn't like facing the wall. After lunch I would relocate the table so I could have some broader view – out the rear window perhaps. *Rear Window*. James Stewart. A real memory. That buoyed me up a bit.

I did up my dishes – rinsed them off and set them in the sink to air dry. I had forgotten to purchase dish soap and towels and was genuinely pleased that I wasn't bothered by it.

I took the two new books to the recliner and began reading the one about obtaining an identity. I had developed some thoughts about it myself and was interested to see that I had come very close to the primary method suggested there in those 'learned' pages. The *learned* tag had been intended as a put down, I suppose. That had been inappropriate. The book contained information essential to my survival so at that moment ranked with the classics.

I won't go into detail about the ID obtaining process since the purpose of this piece is neither that of being a survival manual for other lost souls nor a confession of any marginally legal activities in which I may have found it necessary to indulge. I hurt no one. I took advantage of no one. I found a way to survive – to obtain a job so I could stay off the welfare rolls, out of soup kitchens, pay taxes and feel good about myself. When I earned more money than I needed at the moment, I saw that most of it was placed in the hands of those needier than I. I feel no guilt about what I did. It allowed me to conserve the bank roll, which accompanied me out of the fog, and let it become my back-up or escape fund should that become necessary (again?).

I took the money-filled socks out of the pillow's case where they had been stashed and locked them into the new briefcase. I would now keep it with me at all times – except when facing check points – not trusting hiding places to which others had key access. The tumbler combination needed to be set. There were three, thumb turned, tumblers at each lock so I needed a total of six numbers. What combination should I choose? I realized it was only to provide protection from the casual burglar. An ax or chisel or Swiss Army Knife would make short work of entering it.

I had no number series that was of significance to me – no birth date, no wedding date, no child's birth date. I chose numbers representing my foreseeable, future, age decades – 60, 70, 80. 607080 would be the combination and just to add some finesse I would run it right to left. Once that was set, I felt more secure. I hid ten, one hundred dollar bills under a flap in my wallet so I would have some emergency money on me should I get separated from my briefcase. I disliked basing

33

my life on worst-case scenarios but for the time being it seemed the safest way to go.

After two weeks in the motel – with nary an iota of progress in my search for myself – I found a less expensive apartment in an old, three story, house not far away. It provided a good deal more space – two large rooms, kitchenette, and bath. The manager lived on the third floor. Two couples lived on the second. Mine was on the first. The basement was the day sanctuary for a billion, ill-mannered, night roaming, roaches. I slept under a sheet for the sole purpose of keeping them off my body at night. It seldom worked. I encased my food in plastic, snap-lid, containers. The place was unpleasant but cheap and again required no ID. I soon understood that with no ID, 'utilities furnished' was going to be an essential element in my rental plans.

During the three months I remained there I arranged for an identity, which, though too shallow to set up a bank account or obtain a state ID card, got me by (library cards and such). Due to my particular circumstances and a specific state requirement for a card, I was unable to obtain full, state certified, identification but I had enough to be employable. I held that possibility in reserve for several months while I tried one of the suggestions in the second book – building of all things, briefcases. I contacted a supply company listed in the book, ordered in the crucial parts – hinges, locks, handles, glue, instructions, and so on – and a week later was plying my new trade. I was handy with tools – over a hundred dollars worth – and really enjoyed the activity. I bought cloth remnants from a nearby fabric outlet, with which I covered them. I made some rather good looking pieces. The amount of time one each required reduced my hourly wage to a pittance but it was a start.

While there, I finally opened the yellow and black book and began my adventure with the computer. I started writing stories to keep myself occupied. They flowed naturally and weren't half bad. Perhaps I was a writer. I took frequent, long walks, composing silly, old-fashioned, bumpity, bump, bump, rhyming verses as I made my way around the neighborhood.

34

Spitting

Boy, how I used to love to spit
When five or six or so.
And I must say, was good at it.
As little spitters go.

I spat again the other day.
'Twas great! It really flew!
I hit that target straight away.
(My dentures hit it, too!)

Several months later I rented a much nicer, insect-free, three room apartment above a three car garage. It overlooked a well kept back lawn behind a friendly white house in an old, not quite middle class, neighborhood, with generally happy, laughing, children on every corner. The landlords were friendly but not nosey or inquisitive. The rent was one hundred a month plus twenty-five for utilities.

There were several tense moments during the actual rental process. I felt the urgent need to change my name and leave Jim Johnson a safe distance behind. The ID I had acquired was in the name of Jerry Wilson. I had rented the previous place under the Jim Johnson name, so the good references I had from there – required by the new landlords – would not survive the first call. I made some creative preparations.

I 'fixed' the cover page of a short story I had written so it read: *by Jim Johnson (penname of Jerry Wilson)*. I explained that when I came to town I was writing and giving programs under the penname (not really a falsehood) and had rented the temporary place under that name. Since my former landlord at Roach Haven was also a well known local minister who 'knew' I was a writer, that call helped things work out fine in the end.

I felt the need for a telephone – for safety sake more than anything else. Without solid, picture ID, that was impossible. I spoke with the wife half of the landlord team and explained the personal documents I had sent for had not yet arrived and as a result I couldn't get a phone that I needed to sell my brief cases (so I could pay my rent was implied though not said). She agreed to co-sign for me. I agreed to place a sum equal to three months of phone bills into her safe keeping. Two days later I had a phone (and because I got that one, I never again had a problem getting a telephone or any other utility service). Later I learned that had I applied for TV cable, no ID would have been required and I could have then used that as my reference to obtain phone and other services. I learned gradually about how to survive in my new life.

I alternated mornings writing and afternoons building cases. Earlier I had learned how to ride the bus – fold a dollar bill in fourths, stick it in the slot beside the driver, pull the cord when I wanted off, and never leave home without the schedule. It was plainly something I had never done. My life must have been confined to smaller communities.

Early on, I had taken a bus trip to the mall and visited the Sears store. The cards I had did indeed fit one of their word processors – one of their more expensive models. I explained my dilemma to the young clerk. He called his supervisor over – a smiley, rotund, arms out, little lady who I fully expected to administer a lingering, rib-crushing, bosom busting, hug. She didn't. I breathed easier though still reeked of her perfume for hours. I re-explained things.

"I have these six cards that I understand can only be read on this word processor."

I touched the demo unit on the shelf.

"I need to see what's on them and perhaps print what I find there. Is there anyway we can work something out?"

"I'll tell you what," she said patting my arm. "You buy a ream of paper from us and you can print to your hearts content."

"You are very generous. I expect to pay for ribbon and such."

"Just tell your friends and neighbors about how Sears goes above and beyond for its customers and we'll consider things more than even. Do you need help operating it?"

"Apparently not."

I reached under the left side and pulled a hidden lever. It

hummed to life. I pushed a button and turned a knob and inserted the first card. Away things went. The young clerk arrived with the paper and I handed over a five to pay for it. He left to the register. Either it was a very user-friendly device or I had a good deal of practice operating it. Some of both perhaps but it was obvious I had used one like it.

Each card contained two short stories, written in rhyme. They were for preschoolers and starred *Cricket and His Friends* in twelve adventures – well, eleven adventures and one indoor crafts book. I was impressed. On every page was a space marked 'picture here'. There were no pictures, of course. I was amused at the author's name – The Bashful Bard from # 1 Daffodil Drive, Hidden Valley, USA. At the center of each book was a four-page, pull-out, Parent's Guide. It held suggestions about engaging the child in conversations about life, living, social relations, and being a good person. There were vocabulary building activities and simple experiments they could carry out together. All of that revolved around the content and topic of the particular book. In many ways it was a mental health series. I had to wonder why, of all my probable possessions, I had selected these to bring along. I felt certain I had written them – especially the parent guides. I could predict next elements.

I printed copies, thanked the clerk and his supervisor, and made a mental note that if I ever had the books published I would try to get copies to them.

Beneath my garage apartment, was a small room, which the landlord let me use for my case building. In truth, as much as I enjoyed it, the business never really had a chance. As it turned out my cases were slow to sell. It required that I peddle them to outlets and I found I really hated that part of the activity. I was clearly not a salesman. I made the effort because my livelihood depended on it, but I hated it. One of the other tenants in the first house – second floor – showed some interest in being the middleman – the dealer. I set her up with five units and never heard from her again – nor did her boyfriend. So much for me as a good judge of character! The heavier, wood-base units like I made were on the way out being replaced by the lighter weight, soft side, and aluminum base units. All in all I racked up a significant net loss on that project.

I was lonely. My apartment had been well kept and there was not so much as a wayward roach to play with. Well, there was that little red ant that I coxed onto a pencil and turned it providing him with an endless journey. I tired of it before he did. Maybe a part time real job would provide some companionship. If I chose my spot carefully I figured I could maintain a low profile. I got a paper and perused the help wanted section passing up the ad for a newsreader on a local radio station. I had always been told I had a distinctive voice and feared it might get recognized by the bad guys.

The library had a Stack Assistant opening. I interviewed. Clearly the man in charge was waiting for a young, perky, female-type, far better stacked than I. I was willing to give perky a go, but felt certain I'd bomb out on the other criteria.

A copy center advertised for a copy editor. What they really wanted was somebody with lots of experience doing Apple graphics. I had eyeballed an Apple computer once but doubted if that qualified me.

The last little tear sheet I'd wrested from the paper was an Italian restaurant looking for kitchen help. It happened to be the second restaurant I had seen my first day – the one across the busy street from the bank. I peered through the tinted window and saw no activity – it was about ten thirty a.m. I shrugged and walked away. Then – I don't know why – I retuned and tried the door. It opened. I entered. The well lit kitchen was at the far end of a long, narrow, semi-darkened, dining room. It was pleasant and spotless. The feeling was a comfortable fit to what I was after. A young, attractive, waitress met me half way to the rear.

"We open at eleven, Sir."

She was pleasant.

"I'm here to inquire about the ad for kitchen help."

She smiled. I wasn't sure if it was intended to be friendly or to cover her amusement at my statement.

"Sal's the owner. That's him on the stool."

Sal was a mid-thirties, very Italian, nice looking man.

38

He sported an easy, full-out smile.

"He's here about the job," the waitress announced.

Clearly I wasn't what he expected. Some of the kitchen help was within view across the pass-through window. They were young men – teens and early twenties. Sal offered his hand and indicated the stool beside him at the short counter, which faced rear toward the kitchen. I sat.

"Ever done kitchen before?" he asked

"Only my wife's and quite honestly she kept asking me to leave it," I said hoping to maintain his interest in a way that a flat out 'no' might not have. "Actually, I'm a writer. I'm looking for something that will drag me away from my computer a few hours a day and help me re-enter the realm of real people again."

He extended his smile.

"My wife's a writer for the paper."

"What an intelligent choice you made – a writer," I said trying to match him smile for smile and continue my upbeat approach."

"Only pays minimum," he said, somewhat sheepishly, I thought.

"More to keep busy than to get rich, like I said."

It was not entirely a fabrication. I looked around and asked.

"A family place?"

I had assumed the young waitress might be his daughter or niece or such. Daughter would have been a stretch age-wise although I had been given to understand that Italian boys matured early. It gave me a private smile that I would not share.

"How do you get on with kids?"

He nodded in the direction of the pass-through.

"Love kids. My wife and I had lots of foster sons not a whole lot younger than your crew, there."

I hoped that had not been a fabrication. It came so naturally. Another memory trace, perhaps?

"Give me your number and I'll call early next week," he said. "I have several more applicants to interview."

I understood that he really meant, "Give me some time

to get my head around the idea of having an old guy like you in my youthful kitchen." I handed him a sheet of paper that I'd prepared with essential information. It was typed. He looked impressed. Not too impressed I hoped. I learned another lesson that morning. Fit yourself to the station of the work for which you are applying. I hadn't done that very well considering my tie, tucked in shirt, pressed slacks, and typed info on watermarked stationery. I'd probably end up taking the good lesson rather than getting the job, that time.

I continued to putter a bit at the case making, though mostly for my own entertainment. I gave them away. I again considered growing a beard but settled for a mustache. During large portions of most days I seemed to have found a way to minimize my generalized anxiety level though not my growing loneliness.

It was during those times when my mind was not fully engaged that it rushed back to remind me that things really weren't fine. It was bad at mealtime and at its worst just after I got into bed at night. I usually took an early afternoon nap – thirty minutes or so. I was not so bothered by it then. Maybe that was because it was day or light, or because I was on a couch or that I knew I would only be defenseless for half an hour rather than eight. For whatever reason that was how it was.

I remained suspicious of strangers – especially those whose path I'd cross more than once. That was cause for immediate panic. Were they watching me?

The door at the bottom of the stairs had secure locks, which I kept always locked. I added two sturdy slide bolt latches and a chain lock to the door at the top of the stairs. I bought variegated blue, open weave, drapes for the several windows and left the upper half open to take advantage of the light and the view. I covered the bottom halves with bar curtains and the windows behind them with aluminum foil. Although it was mostly for privacy it also added some degree of insulation value. It was December when I moved in. When summer came I would consider getting an air conditioner. I would need to begin saving my pennies. My expenses just about matched what would soon become my $390.00 a month income.

I began my first novel – well, what I had to assume was my first novel. I had no idea if I had written others. I began not with a plot or even a set of characters but with a title that appeared out of the blue. I wanted to try my hand at a mystery. (Seemed a natural genre for me at the moment!) The title that guided its development was, *"The Murder No One Committed."* It presented a fascinating dilemma for an author and I seemed to love that. I let it stew for a day or so and gradually little possibilities began taking shape. I jotted each of them down on a strip of paper – a third of a sheet. As each bit developed further I added the information in cryptic fashion to the slip, often growing to two or more slips stapled together.

Before week's end I had nearly one hundred slips. I began organizing them – suggesting a chronology. The main character became a renowned retired police detective – late seventies, rotund, and sporting an obstreperous, over sized, mustache. Hmm. He looked a lot like me. I gave him a dry, pun-prone, wit and a reserved, compassionate, helpful, personality. He was single, which freed him to roam from mystery to mystery. It seemed I had a series in mind. (Eventually it grew to a series of more than a dozen novels.)

I loved crafting it. I loved writing it. I loved developing characters and being a mystery writer. It was an easy going, less than intense, brain-stretching, sort of story. The plot grew beyond the murder at hand and allowed the old detective – Raymond Masters as he came to be known – to solve some related cold cases as well. It was the most fun I could remember ever having. There *was* a murder and *no one* had committed it! Despite being formulaic in format – unexpected murder where Masters happened to be, his ferreting out and ruminating through a pile of clues, and his gathering the principals together in the final scene and amazing them with his solution – I believed it worked well.

Publishers apparently didn't – at least not the ten to which I submitted it. I then put it on the shelf for a while being able to think of it as their loss not my failure. (I just kept liking me more and more!) I liked the story and had enjoyed

41

writing it. That may have been its purpose.

I set fiction aside and began a parenting book – *'The One Rule Plan for Family Happiness'*. It literally flowed from my fingers onto the computer screen. Two hundred plus pages finished in four weeks. I diddled with it here and there for a fifth and it soon met with my approval.

It was not until that point that I realized it would not be saleable to a publisher. The author had no verifiable credentials or degrees to make him an authority. I had no resources to have it printed myself nor did I have a distribution network. The big guys had the market cornered. Vanity publishers were also out of my price league.

I hit on an idea and purchased a tape recorder that had the capacity to duplicate tapes – one at a time and only at double speed but it would be a start. I then recorded the book – a laborious, time consuming process – and made copies. I ordered a few tape binders – open at the spine cases that held the needed six, forty-five minute, tapes. I printed large, front and rear, cover-like, stick-on labels. Under my name I added, "Family Consultant". For the less informed that should add the prestige needed to help it sell. I placed a few copies in bookstores and even sold some. Stores needed barcodes so I purchased the necessary software. Bookstores needed ISBN's (International Standard Book Numbers). I registered my new publishing company and paid in advance for my prefix and a small consignment of numbers. Suddenly I was a publisher, official in every sense.

At the level of day to day living, I was taken by the ignorance of the adults there in the neighborhood. By that I mean their total lack of knowledge about important topics such as child rearing, interpersonal relationships, money management, forming and living by a set of positive social values. *Taken by,* was the wrong phrase. *Appalled at* was more nearly akin to my response. I began taking evening strolls and stopping to chat on front porches and in back yards. I took a patient, non-invasive, approach, merely reinforcing what I heard that seemed appropriate or perhaps just a step more appropriate than some other comment had been. Eventually I offered copies of the taped parenting program to those who showed an interest and helped a few set up monthly budgets.

Those folks did not trust professionals – *period*. I therefore did my best to come from a non-professional base. "How do you know so much about kids?" "My wife and I raised lots of foster children. Along the way I learned what helped them turn into well-adjusted, productive, young adults." Most bought that. I also began tutoring some of the children, mostly so I could have some one-on-one time with them nurturing their developing personalities. I didn't take money but readily accepted cookies, casseroles, and such. They didn't want something for nothing. Pride in academic accomplishment took hold where it had not lived before. I was pleased.

I understood my influence was affecting just a tiny enclave. That was fine. Considering my precarious personal situation, I had given up on saving the world. Low key and local had become the required way of life for me.

Eventually there would be other books but that is for later. Back to that kitchen job that I was so sure I had blown. Two weeks later I got a call from Sal.

"Can you begin in the morning? Ten thirty. Like I said, minimum wage and I'm afraid the only fringe benefits you'll get here are free soda and half off on any meals you buy."

"I can live with all of that. Ten thirty it is. Casual dress I assume."

I was suddenly enthused, if a bit anxious, about this new phase in my . . . what? . . . *adventure*, I supposed.

The next morning I awoke to a thunderstorm – odd for that time of year. Later I heard that more rain fell between ten and noon that day than had ever been recorded there in such a span of time. It became my fate to fight my way through the torrent to my first day on the job. I carefully rolled up a pair of spare pants and secured them inside a kitchen trash bag, extended my umbrella, and trudged out into the churning elements. It was a ten-block trek. In addition to my pants, my shoes and socks were also soaked. I wrung out my socks, changed pants, and began work.

My job was to receive the tickets as they came in from

the wait staff and call out to the others the items on each one. Then, when they were ready, I would add sauces, help assemble the dishes according to tickets, and set them in the pass-through for delivery.

It was more difficult for me than it might sound. I had definitely not come from an Italian background. I didn't know a stuffed ravioli from rigatoni. I had never felt so dumb and out of my element in my life. I admired the skill the kids demonstrated and the way they could pick and choose and remember what they needed from what I called. They worked together like the proverbial well-oiled machine. We would often be working a dozen tickets at a time and it was seldom that any of them ever missed a beat. I was amazed and really impressed. My appreciation for kitchen help everywhere grew immensely that first day. Finally, the longest three hours of my life ended.

"You got off 'til four," Sal said. "Then be back for the evening. You'll make up salads ahead."

I hadn't realized I had enlisted for both meals but decided to give it a try. It had become a challenge. I had learned another good lesson that day. I had to tone down my preferred, natural, vocabulary, or I could never be accepted by the others. (Cut the pretty talk an' git down wit da boys.) I kept relatively quiet for the next several days, making mental notes of the grammar and other idiosyncrasies that defined the acceptable kitchen language pattern.

Sal got by with a higher level of language structure because he was the boss. I assumed there had been some education in his background. He interested me. I liked him immediately. I could tell that he was amused at my attempts to speak the kitchen vernacular although he never mentioned it.

He allowed no swearing, and shady stories had to be related without many of the words usually included. I soon came to understand there were only four topics that really interested the boys enough to talk about: their sexual exploits (well inflated I hoped), music and the devices required to play it, vehicles, and money. I mostly just listened. They tried out all their words on me and related the most intimate of

44

romantic details in order to check me out. I seemed to have passed their scrutiny. Before long I had become the go to guy when personal problems surfaced. I liked that role. It was comfortable and I believed I was able to make a positive difference in at least some of their lives.

Sometimes after a long, evening, stroll and talk with one of them, I'd hold out my hand and say, "A hundred dollars please." They would grin, thinking it was a good joke. I would sigh, imagining that at one time in my life it had not been a joke. During the eighteen months I worked there I met and dealt with more life and death situations than I care to count. It tended to keep my mind off my own situation. Aside from Sal, the place was populated by chronically maladjusted people, few of whom had any idea there were things that could be done to make life significantly better for them.

When any two of them agreed on the likely truth of some opinion it immediately became fact in their scheme of things and they proceeded – often dangerously – as if it were true. How youngsters could complete high school and know so little about the important aspects of life – *actually, about anything –* simply dumbfounded me. It was frightening. It would become the basis for further investigation and eventually another book, *"A Crisis of Myths"*. Its premise is that when people base living their lives on Myths (such as unfounded opinions) terrible things are bound to happen for them. My observation was that virtually all of these 'lower station' people lived that way. I referred to them, with greatest respect, as 'the common man'. (I spent a good amount of my non-salad-and-sauce time conducting the research, constructing self-help programs, and demonstrating to educators and mental health professionals how they could markedly improve their offerings. Oddly, even absolute proof that education could become successful and counseling could become both attractive and effective fell pretty much on deaf ears. I was bitterly disappointed with those who held the future of our society in their non-compassionate, non-forward looking, unbelievably defensive, hands."

I would hear, "It can't be done with these kinds of kids."

I would say, "But, look, this is what the kids and I just

45

accomplished. It can be done."

"Maybe *you* can do it but it probably can't be duplicated buy the run of the mill teacher (or therapist)."

"Then get rid of those run of the millers."

"Then system would collapse. Thank you for your interest."

It meant please leave and stop rocking our boat. They smiled in a most condescending manner, patted me on my head, and escorted me to the door. It was disgusting and deeply disturbing.

(That book details the year I spent on that project so I won't go on into it further here.)

I ramble. I soon became kitchen manager, which meant I came in early to prep things and make sauces, and locked up at night. It took up most of my time. I became close with Sal and his wonderful young family. There was a running joke among his extended family members regarding their nebulous, probably remote, ties to the Italian crime families bearing the same last name. There did seem to be some truth in the tie if not any actual mutual activities. If bad guys were indeed after me, the possibility of Italian crime family ties was unsettling. It eventually made my association with the restaurant fully uncomfortable.

In the end, my discomfort grew to the point I could no longer tolerate it. My initial paranoia returned. I became suspicious of every patron that looked the least bit Mediterranean. I made excuses so I wouldn't have to be present at gatherings that included parents and brothers. I felt as though I were gasping for breath – hopefully not one of my last. I felt the noose tightening. I began keeping the light on all night. I would check and recheck the locks. I kept away from windows. I hated to answer the phone for fear it would be a 'bad guy'. It *could* have been the Mafia that was after me. Night after night I walked those long blocks home in the blackness of unlit side streets. It was twenty minutes of thoroughgoing terror. I had to leave.

The whole thing seemed like such a full-blown overreaction. Did part of me know something it wasn't telling me outright?

CHAPTER THREE:
The horrific journey through my subconscious

A brief recap: Well settled into my apartment, my new job, and my live – such as it was – I turned my full private focus toward discovering my past. All the usual methods for dealing with a fugue – amnesia about ones identity and past plus flight away from ones home base – had produced nary an iota of progress. To wait it out is preferred method number one. Over those six months, nothing had come of waiting. Such states typically last no more than a few weeks at the most. A few have been known to last much longer, of course. Trying to tie my personal past to my professional expertise produced no results – except that one fleeting image of the boy sitting on the couch and *it* had really just been volunteered from someplace deep inside. Not even the most time honored method of all, pummeling my temple with the ball of my hand, had helped me remember.

I established a plan. Step one was to review everything I knew about self-hypnosis. Step two was to practice age regression techniques and establish a process by which I could be assured that my thoughts would be available afterwards. I settled on verbalizing my thoughts aloud while in a hypnotic state and capturing them on tape. It worked well as I practiced – the physical process of speaking and recording, I mean.

I was well aware that such a regression technique produced dubious and often unreliable results. The deepest part of the mind – fully illogical and perfectly obedient – has one characteristic that is both positive and negative. It does its very best to find out what you want it to do and then it puts all of its energy toward accomplishing that end. One can see how wishful thinking could easily sabotage the process. I tried to clear myself of foregone conclusions – something else I realized I really couldn't accomplish.

I quickly discovered I was so familiar with the process that I had certainly used it with my patients.   I must have found it useful or surely I would not have wasted our time pursuing it.   Those disclaimers in place, I really had no alternative, regardless of the questionable success rate. I felt confidant that if the picture I dredged up was inaccurate, I would recognize it or feel the dissonance it created as I contemplated its legitimacy.

In my practice sessions, I always began with the vision of that black apple. It had come with me so might – should – have some strong ties to my psyche of old. I counted on that, in fact.   I would recline on the couch, head and shoulders elevated on a pillow for ease of breathing and talking. I placed the microphone on my chest and turned on the recorder.   I would take three, deep, lung-renewing breaths, and close my eyes.   I spoke every command, every response, and every thought out loud.

The process was simple, but required precise application. Reclining comfortably, with eyes gently closed and arms in a comfortable position, I focused on the black apple for some time, allowing my muscle groups to relax.   That occurred all quite automatically.   Tense muscles commandeer the part of the mind one needs to access in this type of exercise.   In so doing it is as if they put a strangle hold on the passage into the deep mind narrowing it so nothing can enter and nothing may leave. My self-talk proceeded in the following manner.

Relax.   Open my mind and allow it to work for me. Focus only on what I have to say. It is safe here now. Remove all concerns other than relaxing and focusing on what I have to say. Slip deeper and deeper and deeper relaxed. Remain alert but focused on my every word – my ever request. More and more relaxed.   More and more focused.   The world

48

outside my mind grows quiet, safe, and insignificant as I relax and focus. I am in search of that which was me some time ago. It has become hidden in the deepest part of my mind and I must focus my search there. I must enter and explore the deepest part of my mind. Relax the barricades. Open the doors. It is only I who will peek inside. It is only I who will learn from those depths what resides there. Relax. Focus on this most important undertaking. I will remember all that I see and hear. I will accurately relate out loud every nuance of this experience.

Now, I will move back along my life path. It is as if the pages of calendars are turning in the breeze, revealing days, months, years now past, finding the very moment that I request. Go back now. Go back to _____ .

All I then would have to do was to add the specific place in time and the visions should begin to flow immediately, much like rewinding a video tape to a specified spot and then engaging playback.

The first time that I worked on things in a fully serious way, I set my head to relive my life during the month just prior to my appearance in Joplin. My thinking was that should bridge the gap between now and then. I gave it my best effort but my mind remained silent. After thirty minutes I roused, fully confused. Perhaps recent memories were too forcefully tied to the reason for my amnesia and would therefore be the most difficult to reopen. I had believed just the opposite but saw the logic in my new perspective.

I then set my mind for my 47th birthday which I believed was a full five years before. I assumed that beginning that far back, there would be no tie-in at all with the later causal trauma.

My, was I mistaken!

What happened next had no hook in time but it was the most mentally gut wrenching experience I could imagine ever encountering.

The images were perfectly clear – sharp, focused, panoramic. I saw what had to be my waiting room – maybe fifteen by twenty, newly furnished with two heavy couches and two matching chairs. There was a wooden rocker in one

49

corner and a small wooden table with two chairs in another. There were book and magazine racks and a toy box. The room had honey oak wainscoting up about three feet and a blue, beige, and red wall paper above it. The ceilings were gray paneling with beams. A lazy, slowly rotating, ceiling fan added motion to the setting. The room was lighted by six pin up lamps offering soft but sufficient illumination. The low nap on the light brown carpet added texture and coziness to the setting. All in all it was a pleasant, inviting, relaxing room.

My office mirrored it next door. It was as long but no more than ten feet wide. At one end was a low built-in bookcase. There was a door in one corner that led to my living quarters and one opposite it on the diagonal that led into the waiting room. The blue sofa backed against the wall shared with the waiting room. Two blue, swivel rockers sat opposite it. A table – for testing, I assume – sat in an alcove at the end opposite the bookcase. Again pin up lamps provided the soft, friendly, source of light. Other features mimicked the waiting room. There was a large, pleasingly proportioned picture above the sofa the details of which I could not make out. A landscape, perhaps.

There was a large entry/secretarial area to the east of the waiting room with a long, gently inclining, ramp leading up to the restrooms. A hall ran south with two smaller rooms off to the left. At its end it opened into a large meeting room – the sign on the door read, "Mill Room". It seemed to be forty by fifty, carpeted, with a vaulted ceiling and a floor to ceiling mural of a mill and gently cascading water on the east wall.

After my mental tour I felt myself relax more deeply than I had remembered experiencing before. It flooded me with calm and happiness – security. That lasted about as long as it took me to relate it, here.

Then, there came that precisely animated vision that would revisit me night after night for the rest of my days. It began in a seemingly benign fashion. First, I must furnish background from visions that emerged in irregular, concurrent flashes. So much was rushing in on me I struggled to verbalize it all.

I was, as must seem obvious, a clinical psychologist. I specialized in children, adolescents, and their families. One of my young patients – fourteen, short for his age, handsome in that black hair, brown eyed, young Italian way – came to see me weekly, being driven the hour and a half from the south Chicago area. His limo also brought his mother, a male, driver, and a three hundred pound, seriously serious, closed mouthed, bodyguard. He was black. I mention it because it later seemed to play a tangential part in things.

Soon into our relationship the boy revealed that his father was a part of organized crime – a secondary boss in a large family-based business. I told him it was best that he not go on about it. He insisted, claiming that was at the basis of his problem – depression over the things he had learned his father, uncles, and older brothers were doing. With his permission I included his mother in the discussion. She agreed that her son should share whatever he felt he needed to share. She, too, was at her wits end about it and would have left the family with her son in a minute had it been allowed. That was not a possibility, of course – not so long as the 'family' stayed in business

Several weeks later the two of them entered my office together with a plan, of sorts, to present to me. They would continue to share with me secrets of family 'doings' and I was to pass them on to federal authorities to shut the family down – put the father and his colleagues behind bars. The mother handed me addresses and phone numbers of the appropriate agencies – some specific to agents names. She had done her homework. I believed it proved the sincerity of her commitment. It was the only way they felt the two of them could ever be free of the 'Mafia' cloud. Considering the horrific deeds that were revealed to me and the massiveness of the operation, I agreed. My inner essence trembled. We continued in that fashion for a number of months.

I didn't ever have to testify. My information had been enough to allow the authorities to gather the data they needed. My agreement was that I was to be kept off the record completely.

My hypnotic revelations continued.

51

One evening, after my parade of patients had passed for the day, I was winding down, straightening up the waiting room. I heard the outside door open but not close. Presently two large men entered. One stood at the door and the other entered the room. I recognized them as being the men who typically accompanied the boy from the crime family. They never looked friendly but that evening no trace of friendly appeared on their faces or graced their body language. The larger one, the body guard, the scarier of the two, spoke.

"I have this message from Tony (the boy's father). Listen carefully. It's about you talking private family stuff to the Feds. He's giving you one day to leave town and never showin' yourself nowhere again. If you don't leave or if we can find you if we decide to come lookin', your family and patients will meet with very unfortunate happenings – intensive care, long term rehab, disfiguration, caskets. You get my drift, Doc?"

"I get the picture."

My mouth went dry and my throat tightened. I found it difficult to speak though I continued.

"It will be impossible for me to find other therapists for all my patients in that amount of time."

"Your patients are of no concern to us."

"I can take my wife and son with me, of course."

"You will fly solo. You cannot take them and you cannot tell them. You can never contact them again once you're gone. That's the point." He managed a short lived, sinister, smile. "The worst punishment Tony could devise for a sonofabitchin', sentimental, traitor, slob like you. If you tell anybody anything about your whereabouts or about the aforementioned 'stuff' your family are dead."

"Certainly we can discuss this and find some alternative."

"Nobody don't *discus* with Tony. Leave! Now! Never let your ass be seen or heard from again."

They left as quickly as they had arrived. The outside door clicked shut. I sank into the rocker struggling to come to grips with the ramifications of this sudden, horrifying, turn of events. I replayed it all in my head. 'Without informing my family or patients about why I was leaving I was just to leave permanently and live the rest of my life in anonymity. Not doing so would result in terrible consequences for my family and patients.' The reality began to set in. My soul drained. Emptiness and anguish welled up. It was unfair. Of course, that was the point. It presented an unsolvable dilemma. Of course, that was the point. It suggested the greatest possible loneliness and despair for all of us. Of course, that was the point. It generated the greatest fear I had ever known. Of course, . . .

From there the images are confused for a while and lose their chronology. Bits and pieces floated in and out. The bank. Cash. Large amounts of cash. Packing a bag and clandestinely depositing it in the trunk of my car. Being with my wife that one last time and upsetting her because she sensed something was terribly wrong.

As I lay there on the couch in the safety of my garage apartment, I sensed my chest heaving and tears streaming down my cheeks.

Suddenly there was no safety.

The images became clear and organized again allowing the ugly brutality of it all to arrive well focused. I saw myself driving home the following evening thinking "one day" meant sometime during the day following my encounter with Big Scary and Bigger Scary. I would extend it as long as possible and be gone by midnight. No more than twenty-five hours had elapsed.

There were flashing red lights just ahead down the road. It looked to be near my rural home. An accident, I figured. That curve was deceptively sharp and many a teen driver had ridden the back of an ambulance away from the spot.

It was not an accident. There were a dozen police cars and EMT vans in my driveway and crowded together along the road just in front. A sheriff's car. A state trooper. Several city police units. Others. I had to park a half block away. I hurried toward the house. One of the local officers recognized me and intercepted me, holding me firmly in his arms.

"You don't want to go up there, Doc. I'm sorry. But it's best if you stay here."

I broke loose and ran toward the area inside the circular driveway. The grass was red – with blood I imagined. Two figures lay on the lawn, covered in black plastic sheets. Two other officers restrained me as I neared them.

"You live here?" one asked.

"Yes. This is my place. What's going on?"

"I sure hate to be the messenger in this one, Doctor Blabla. But it's your wife and son. They were gunned down right here about thirty minutes ago. Strangely, it has all the trappings of a syndicate hit. I am so sorry."

He offered his open arms and shoulder and pulled me close as I began sobbing uncontrollably.

After a time the detective in charge came over and repeated condolences.

"When you can, tomorrow, come in and let's see if we can sort this thing out. Autopsies are automatic in cases such as this. Can I have an officer take you somewhere – to a friend's place?"

I shook my head.

"I need to see them."

"Not a good idea. Looked to be long blasts from old fashioned machine guns. Devastating and fully untraceable."

"I *will* see them. You coming or staying here?"

He walked with me and bent down to lift back the black shrouds. First my wife and then my son. They were horrific images – images I had to see and images that would follow me into my later darkness and awaken me screaming night after night for years and years and years.

The detective went on.

"It's probably little solace but after your wife was shot, it appears your son tried to come to her assistance. He took most of the fire."

It was not solace, of course, though it was exactly what he would have done. There could be no solace under such fully horrendous circumstances. I went inside and up to my study. I watched from behind the curtains as the ambulances carried my life away. I collapsed on the couch and sobbed myself to sleep.

My next memory is my emergence in Joplin. Things fell

54

into place. The trigger for my amnesia suddenly seemed both obvious and reasonable. The brief expedition into the depths of my memory re-established the horror and I awoke there in my new apartment to a still heaving chest and tear drenched shirt and pillow case. I immediately stood as if planting my feet firmly on the floor might help or was in some other way the reasonable thing to do. I just stood there motionless for many minutes. I re-ran the images, interested that *they* had followed me into consciousness. My name had not, even though I remember it having been spoken. The tape recording had not been necessary that time though later I did review it for details.

I found myself nodding as if my present mind was verifying or at least accepting the recent revelations. Although the 'known' aspects of the experience were devastating it was the unknown that seemed to be prolonging my tears. Had patients also been harmed? What turn had the course of their therapy taken? How old would they be now? What were their names? Just when did that actually take place? Just prior to my arriving in Joplin, I had to assume. What arrangements had been made for my family? By whom? Questions piled high.

Briefly, I focused on how my friends and neighbors must have reacted and interpreted the events. Mafia killers were virtually never caught. Could my immediate disappearance have been interpreted to mean I was in on it? Most likely folks would think the purpose had been to wipe out my entire family and that I was now wearing concrete boots at the bottom of a lake somewhere. They would have to wonder what my affiliation had been with organized crime. It could taint my reputation. At that point I didn't care, of course. The ruination of my reputation could not compare to the loss of all that I loved and treasured.

I began to pace as I thought. I began to understand about my recent overreaction to the Italian connection that circulated among Sal's family. Very likely it was not an overreaction at all. It was at that point I understood that had to leave and do so in such a way that there would be no way – no possibility – for my beloved Joplin 'family' to trace my whereabouts. I did not dare risk even the faintest possibility of putting them in danger.

I devised a story about having pancreatic cancer with only a few months to live. I found I was a convincing actor. I was greatly bothered that it would put them through sadness at the moment but considering the possible, perilous, alternatives I went ahead. For them to have closure at my death should certainly be better than worrying forever where I was, how I was, if I was. Sometimes no alternative is best but still, we have to make a choice.

The other possibility, of course, was that Sal's family had no malevolent connection to me. Still, if my original Cicero nemesis did come looking and did find me, Sal and his wife and children – my loved ones – could become the target of Tony's heartless brutality. I could not chance that either. I could especially not chance that. I doubted if my mind could endure two families being destroyed because of me. I would leave Joplin to die with old friends far away and send a notice of my death later on thus providing finality for them. Should they find me and contact me they could be putting themselves in grave – mortal – danger. I just had to make certain that was avoided.

It all convinced me of one thing. I had to live my life under the assumption that I was being watched by Tony's family. He was in prison (an impression from my hypnotic trip) but his extended family was not. They could be looking for me to slip up – to try and contact somebody from my past, to reveal something about myself that I shouldn't, to appear too happy. I must sever the Joplin connection in such a way that I could never be traced back there. Perhaps another name change. It was becoming increasingly difficult to do that – new laws and background investigative procedures. I kept track of such things the way investors checked the financial page. I would see.

Over the next several weeks I began building the case for my terminal condition – demonstrating symptoms and later taking time off for 'doctor appointments'.

At the same time I continued working on me to dredge up the rest of my past. It had not returned full-blown.

Although monumental in importance and relevance to my present situation the facts revealed up to that point were an infinitesimal part of my total past.

The next session was challenging in many ways. Simply put, I was scared out of my gourd to even try the procedure again. It took three attempts at lying down and trying to relax before I became comfortable enough to proceed. In between, I got up and neurotically rechecked the door and window locks. The terror was real but there was also a flip side. Somewhat humorously as I look back on it, in my first vision of the black apple that day there was a chunk eaten out of it. There may or may not be psychological ramifications to that. I can chuckle about it, now. At the time it riled me more than a little. That apple was like my only friend from my past. It seemed to me that my subconscious was not taking my situation seriously. (I know, it doesn't make a lot of sense to me now, either.) Eventually I 'fixed' the image by rotating it in my mind so the missing chunk was not visible.

Closing my eyes under any circumstances had become terrifying. Closed eyes only happened at night and then only due to my level of sheer exhaustion. That – with the resulting darkened eye sockets, shaking, lack of appetite and rapid weight loss – made my cancer story appear legitimate but it was fully unhelpful in every other way. It was difficult to think clearly and remember even the routine things. My work in the restaurant fell apart – one of the young men even pointed that out to Sal.

On the third attempt, I managed to quickly obtain a very deep level of focused openness (hypnosis). Later I would ascribe that to the immediate escape it promised from the growing horrors of my everyday existence. In some ways it had been ill advised. I might have found it so comforting 'down there' that I would refuse to awaken. Fortunately, that did not occur. What transpired over the next dozen sessions provided the picture of a remarkably unique life. I will collapse those sessions by offering the final reconstruction.

Several days after my second birthday – as that reconstruction went – my parents were preparing Christmas in our house. I had been dispatched to my babysitters down the

57

street for the night. They were an old couple and lived just outside the city limits because Negros and Indians were not allowed to stay in town past sundown. He was Negro – the first free-born son in his family. Age sixty. She referred to herself as Mexican Indian but looked a match to her husband in color if not facial features. She was fifty. They had lost their only son to appendicitis when he was three or so. They loved me and I would soon grow to love them.

That night my parent's house burned and they were killed. My babysitters – The Franklins – took me in and raised me as their own with the unofficial blessing of the town fathers – Manchester, Indiana, population four hundred. "An orphan is a terrible blight on a community," I would later hear the mayor say in reference to me.

My new parents gave me the name Craig and to ease official things, such as school and medical records, I used their last name. I went through school there and later attended the small, church run college that sat at the north eastern edge of the community. Many minute details of my life surfaced that are irrelevant for this rendering, but they added such legitimacy to the story that I recognized it had to be true. Again I wrote of them in the story of my tenth year, *"Zephyr in Pinstripes"*.

We made a unique looking family unit walking to church, Pop in his black suit, Mom in her long white dress, white straw hat, and white gloves, me bobbing, towheaded, between them, my small, lily white hands gentled into there strong, dark ones. No one ever spoke of it within my earshot and I seldom thought about it. At four I remember that I was sorely distressed when I asked Pop when my skin would turn the beautiful color of his and he told me it wouldn't. He said that I should be as proud of my white skin as he was of his black skin. I learned to live with it.

I earned several degrees switching early on from Speech and Drama to psychology, eventually earning graduate degrees, passing state boards, and beginning to practice. Along the way I married my best friend from childhood and taught in several colleges – whether full or part time I still could not be certain. I wrote books, mostly for children as I

58

remembered.

Life with my wife and son was idyllic.

That was the short and sweet essence of LBJ – Life Before Joplin.

It became clear that I could not share the horror of my family member's deaths with others in a fully truthful manner. Yet, I needed to be able to explain their absence in my life. It somehow seemed 'healthier' to me to represent myself as having been a husband and father.

I devised a story that handled that and probably would gain me some immediate compassion from those who learned about it. The latter may not have represented such a healthy need but it eased my initial acceptance in new settings. Still, it seemed to indicate that I sought to be liked and perhaps, even, taken care of.

This was the alternate story I constructed – simple and straight forward. One New Year's Eve while my son and wife were driving to a party they were in an accident and killed by a drunken teen-ager. I was not with them because I was finishing up some work and was to join them later. That was that. They were gone. I was dealing with it in a clearly courageous manner. People immediately developed a soft spot for me.

In life or in that fantasy the same truth supported the story – I had lost my family in a horrendous fashion. I felt no guilt about the modification. Society was changing. Unmarried men were looked upon with suspicion when they chose to be with children or teens. I wanted to continue helping those I had been trained to help. The story worked to make my pure motives legitimate. For some reason that I could not pinpoint, that seemed to be extremely important to me.

Subsequently, I remembered about my sixteenth year and my attempted suicide. The time leading up to it came through so clearly that I revisited it several times with hypnosis and put my memories into the form of a diary that I thought would be helpful to adolescents feeling down about life. (And what teenager doesn't!) It became a book: *"36 Hours To Live: the diary of a teenage suicide."* It chronicles, hour by hour, the thirty six hours leading up to the moment I 'took my life' – as best as I could recreate it. I included my thoughts and reasons and even humorous musings about life and the human condition. It actually turned out to be a very uplifting book which celebrates life. It has been studied by young people in many high schools.

Let me return to my departure from Joplin. I had become extremely attached to Sal and his family as well as to several of the young people I had come to know. Leaving what had grown to become my family of loved ones was an incredibly difficult undertaking. I had waited too long once. I would not risk that again. I put my 'condition' on the fast track and I soon said my goodbyes.

I hired an out of town, part time, mover thinking that would protect my trail – in both directions. A few weeks later I 'died' and the notice was sent via a mail forwarding service. The ruse was only partially successful but no one seemed to have been put in jeopardy – although they could have been.

Deciding on my post-Joplin destination was less difficult than I had anticipated. It was the summer of 1993. I paged through my atlas. North West Arkansas was close. It looked comfortable, with lots of green and blue indicating mountains, streams, lakes, and parkland. All quite clandestinely, I moved to Fayetteville, Arkansas, landing amid the verdant Ozark Mountains and a bevy of imaginatively dedicated Razorback fans. Immediately it felt like home – not a *transient* home like Joplin, but, for some reason, a really *forever* home.

My 'OOOO-PIG-SOOIE" might not ever be fully convincing but it, too, felt right. The need to look over my shoulder whenever I was not in my apartment did not diminish the way I had hoped it would. In most ways I did feel somewhat relieved, but there I was, having to start all over again. How many times would I have to go through this? I imagined fat-bellied, Boss Tony, smoking his Cuban cigar, laughing at me struggling there as he watched in the crystal ball on his table – the one which kept track of my every move – perhaps every thought. Paranoia might be at bay but clearly it had not been fully dispatched.

It posed an impossible dilemma: If he had kept close tabs

on me, hiding produced no margin of safety for me. It *would* raise my minute by minute level of terror, however. If he didn't really care where I was, so long as I remained distraught and eternally frightened, hiding was not helping but would at least lower the terror level. If he didn't know where I was and he wanted to find me to hurt me, hiding was essential, with continued, thoroughgoing terror an unavoidable part of it. I had to live within that third possibility; the others would represent recklessness that I dared not allow.

My first apartment in Fayetteville – quite temporary as it turned out – was on the upper floor of a beautiful old, magnificently maintained, house. There were two large rooms with kitchen facilities along the east side of one of them. My furniture fit perfectly – right down to my two big braided rugs and drapes.

I spent the first two months writing – putting off the job search so I could give my full attention to getting some of what I considered my important thoughts down in black and white. It was during that period in which I finished *The Crisis of Myths*. Soon after arriving in Fayetteville, I awoke one morning, with a fascinating, two-pronged, idea. "Stump People", I was saying to myself. Then, "A positive social philosophy all wrapped as a warm fuzzy story about the 'Stump People'."

Their name eventually became, *The Little People of the Ozark Mountains* who, among other delightful things, hollowed out stumps for their homes. First, I wrote a short, concise, summary of the premise:

The Legend of The Little People of the Ozarks®

In the folklore of the Ozark Mountains, there are fleeting
references to the Little People –
tiny folks, about as tall as a grape hyacinth,
possessed of
magical powers, good cheer, and just a touch of the imp.
Legend has it that they busy themselves
watching over the mortals of the area,
performing good deeds and
granting wishes to those in need.

61

Only rarely do they let themselves be seen by
the Biggins (the mortals), and then,
only to those who believe in them,
and in the powers of love,
unselfish generosity, and
the basic goodness that resides somewhere inside all of us.
They have this magical maxim which, it is said, will bring the
best of life to all who repeat it
three times each and every day:
"If love and trust and helpfulness
Each day we all employ,
We then shall build a World so Blessed,
All lives will flow with joy."
Try it and you, too, will believe.
You will soon come to discover and treasure
your very own Little Person, who
regularly perches himself right there on your shoulder,
ready and willing to offer
counsel, comfort, and courage,
whenever it is needed!

I created two main characters for the story(ies)– Jay, the bright and enthusiastic ten year old mortal boy and Twiggs the twelve and three quarters year old Little Person with a sudden, sad, weight on his shoulders. They enjoyed a wonderful summer together in the meadow and stream behind Jay's country home. They romped in the tall grass, swam in the creek, climbed trees (and small bushes) and did all the other things typical of boys their ages. During the down times they discussed the differences and similarities of their cultures. They discussed life and the proper and improper ways to live it. They grappled with the lessons of history – their two histories – and the apparent unwillingness of grownups in the mortal realm to listen to those lessons the way the Little People did. In the end a terrible, seemingly unsolvable dilemma, loomed large in their lives.

Don't be fooled because the characters are children. These are stories for grownups.

It goes on, but that presents the bare bones of *Book One:*

Ring of the Farjumpers. Three more books have followed in the series. Kids enjoy the stories. Teens and grownups grow from the philosophy – at least that is my intent. I love the characters and how they bring the positive social philosophy to life in what I hope is a non-preachy, down to earth manner. I especially enjoy the positive response I have received every time others have referred to the books in my presence.

I took money from my 'big fund' and had that first book printed – 100 copies with line drawing illustrations, which I fashioned. The story about the drawings was that the boys had made them so I figured they didn't have to be really professional. Surely I could draw as well as ten and twelve year old boys.

Clearly the concept of a positive social philosophy was pressing hard within me. Everything I wrote reeked of it! I suppose since my terror had been set in place by men who gave no heed to the need for such an approach – essential if mankind were to survive much longer – it was reasonable that it should have become so important for me. My mental gut told me it was something more. I had virtually nothing beyond that nebulous, churning feeling. There was an emotion attached – sadness. Not the horrific sadness I was experiencing over the loss of my family but a more gentle, long term, I-should-be-doing-more-than-I-am sort of sadness. Perhaps guilt was tangled in and around the feeling.

I was deeply disappointed that my name had not yet surfaced. It was really the key to so many things. That *not* being present, I did what I could to locate the town that had come up – Manchester, Indiana. It was not clear if that was where I lived at the time of the tragedy. It seemed unlikely. Such a tiny town could not support a clinical psychologist.

To my puzzlement, there was no Manchester, Indiana. There was North Manchester and two really tiny unincorporated places close by that used Manchester in their names. It might have been one of them but descriptive information seemed to be unavailable. North Manchester was way too large to match the place in my memory, although it was home to a church affiliated college, Manchester College. What about that college? I found and perused its website. It was joy with no boundaries when I began churning through the pictures on the site. I recognized Old Main with the tower that housed the clarion. One older residence hall looked familiar. The Oak Leaves was the school paper. I had worked on it. I ran down the list of former presidents. There he was – A. Blair Helman. I could see his tall, chubby countenance delivering the chapel message from behind the podium on the stage in the auditorium. I could see me in my assigned seat. I hoped for at least a few flashes of me doing things – being with friends, in class, anything. Nothing came. It was a sterile memory but it was a memory, documented by after the fact information.

It had no graduate program so my later degrees had to have come from elsewhere. Where might 'elsewhere' have been? Geneseo, New York rang a bell. I looked it up. It was home to an arm of the state university system there and had grown up as a teacher's college. It was a small community set in rolling hills not far from Lake Conesus just west of the Finger Lakes and south of Rochester. That, too, rang a bell. One morning, months later I would awaken understanding that I had taught psychology there right out of graduate school. We had lived out on the lake. Our baby was born while we lived there. Another real memory. Still no names for me, for my wife, or for our son.

One grand memory – image – accompanied the lake setting. I was reclining on my back on the couch and our very new baby was lying on my chest doing pushups – of a sort. He would straighten his arm and raise up. Then he'd reach out to touch my face, losing support and falling, much to his obvious surprise. The most magnificent part of the image was that when he would reach his greatest height and could look me in the face, he would smile. I can see it so clearly and I treasure it to this moment.

What was his name? I want to say Franklin but that was my parent's name. It could be both. When asked, I would use that as his name. For some reason Ginny – short for Virginia, I assumed – seemed right for my wife. It became the name I used when referring to her.

What could it be that allowed so many memories and yet

64

protected the names involved so completely? Perhaps having the name would allow memories to surface that my deep mind didn't think the rest of me could handle. *My* position was that it was frustrating me. *Its* position may have been that it was protecting me. Since ones Deep Mind is always ultimately in control of things it would prevail until I found a key.

That dilemma led me to begin reading the latest research on the subconscious processes – data-based material, not Freudian ramblings. Both the local library and the university library proved to be good resources. The city library was just a few blocks away from where I lived. It soon came to me that I knew as much about the topic as most of the writers. I set out to assemble a therapeutic program based on my previous and recently acquired pieces of information. I was quite certain I had been using a version of the procedure to treat patients. I assumed my new endeavor would prove to be an improvement – rethinking it as I was clearly forced to do during its reconstruction.

Again, it was based on a system of positive values. It provided almost immediate relief from phobias and anxiety that were event specific (attached to some event, person, place, activity). I wrote a script and recorded it like I had done with the parenting book. (Later I published it in book form as: *The Secrets of Deep Mind Mastery* – now in its 4th edition.) As I came to specify its utilization in a wider variety of applications, I tried to apply it to my own situation. It really wasn't intended for such things but with it I was able to keep my terror under better control most of the time. I detached it from its nighttime trigger and became able to walk outside without shaking and hyperventilating. So, as a symptom/ reaction controller it helped significantly. It was far less successful on the amnesia front – well, initially at least, it was really not of any further help at all on that front.

After two months in Fayetteville, I took a job as a clerk in a store. I won't go into details other than to say I found it enjoyable. I had pleasant folks with whom to work, the hours were fine – eleven to five – and it was only five blocks from where I lived. Ninety-five percent of the customers were women so few make me suspicious that they might be Mafia hit men.

I loved the little apartment and soon had fixed it up in a cozy, homey way. A problem developed that required me to leave. In converting the place into apartments, mine and the one below were put on the same forced air system. The gentleman who had lived down stairs for years was a cigar smoker and I could not tolerate that in my air. So, after three months I began searching for an alternative.

I ran across an opportunity to become the manager of a small apartment complex – 20 units. My rent and phone were free. It was like adding four hundred dollars to my monthly income – well, probably more like 250 as I wouldn't have landed in such a posh place if I were paying for it. As a surprise to me, rent in Fayetteville was three times what it had been up north. Still, with that arrangement my finances would be fine. Essentially my 'job' was to rent apartments, bug tenants when payments were late, and check them out, disappointing them with the small amount of their deposit they were getting back. It was hardly my thing but I gave it my best shot. I kept on with my job in the store. I was transferred to run a very small-volume store near the edge of the city. It was a one man operation – 8 A.M. to 5 P.M.

My loneliness grew. My purpose in life became ill-defined. My lessened anxiety gave me rein to do things. I had nothing to do. I had been more productive back in the days of my constant terror. What should – could – I do?

CHAPTER FOUR
Retreat

While at that new store I had lots of time to do other things during the day. By ten a.m. I would have the merchandise straightened up, the floors and doors cleaned, and boredom would set in. I began making small clay pieces – birds, buffalo, Indians, horseman, Indians on horseback hunting buffalo. I offered them for sale. They didn't sell. I guess I had been correct way back at the beginning: There I was sporting a PhD with no saleable skills. Again I smiled.

Being alone and so isolated there in the new store eventually began taking its toll. Soon I found myself back to being in a constant state of unease. Every time a car would pull up outside I would panic expecting unpleasant happenings. I would even see Big Scary and Bigger Scary sitting there inside the cars. Then some dainty little old lady would exit and I would begin breathing again. It was clear I couldn't remain there.

In the end the decision was made for me. The stores were sold and a new management team was brought in. I was out. I had been able to save a considerable amount from what had grown into a substantial six day a week salary. I hated my apartment rental position. I just needed to get away for awhile.

Some dear friends offered a room in there rural home until I could get things settled. They had no idea about the exact nature of those 'things' and were the kind that never pressed. I set aside two thousand dollars and paid it out to them two hundred dollars a month to help with food and whatever other expenses it would cover. It was too little but they never mentioned it. I kept hoping that someday I would be able to make it up to them.

It was while I was there that I wrote, *Red Grass at Twilight*, a fictional rendering of the tragedy that took my family. I had hoped its writing would slip other things into place for me. In many ways it followed my recent life in essence if not in fact. I worked out the story so my terror was removed in the end. It worked well in the story though certainly seemed to remain an impossibility in real life. It's a pretty good story, I think, with a thriller-type ending high atop a – well, that would spoil the story. It was clearly a wish fulfillment piece on my part. The wish remained unanswered.

I also busied myself making clay beads and fashioning them into necklaces and broaches. Hand rolled, hand painted, jewelry. I put them in a flea market to sell. I had very little success. It seemed that no matter what I tried, nobody wanted it. I got discouraged. I took long walks before daylight most every morning. I felt safer in the darkness – it was a match to what I felt inside. I'd walk close to the river and through a woods. I always felt better afterwards.

Eventually the money I had set aside ran low. I needed to get on with my life in a more productive, self-sufficient fashion. The time off had been good for me regardless of the bead fiasco. My patient friends had helped me more than they can ever know.

A job became available as a phone answerer and data input person in a small local manufacturing concern. The owners – friends of my friends – were willing to take a chance on me. I found a relatively inexpensive apartment nearby. It had been my intention to stay just long enough to make my books become a constant source of income, thinking that being in town should make that easier. During the first seven years back in town I finished over sixty novels and had them printed through my publishing company. I love to write and could hardly wait to get home each afternoon and begin

68

plunking away at the keyboard – three to nine most every day. Weekends became round the clock, finger-flying, marathons. Twice, I engaged the services of book marketers but in both instances they proved a failure. Most of that, I tell myself, was due to their incompetence but I have had to wonder if the mediocre quality of my work was also a part of it. Oh, well! *I* like what I write and as I said, I love the process.

Aside from the friends with whom I lived for those eight months, I intentionally built barriers against establishing close relationships. I told myself it was because I didn't dare risk putting others in danger. It was lonely. My best friends became the characters in my stories. When I'd finish a novel I would go through 'character withdrawal' until I was fully engaged with a new set. I don't know if other authors experience that or not.

Then, all quite unexpectedly, a youngster came into my life. He was fourteen, generally unkempt, educationally challenged (though rather bright, I discovered), and clearly willing to form a friendship with an old man. He worked a few hours every Saturday morning cleaning out the dryers in a Laundromat I used. His mother worked there. I spoke to him and smiled the way I speak to and smile at everybody (usually hoping it will go no further). He all but ignored me. That was fine – probably a relief, even. Later, I saw him eyeballing me from across the room. He made an excuse to walk by me and say hello. An oddly suspicious way of approaching somebody now. I never pressed. I responded in some way. He intrigued me.

Week by week the relationship grew – slowly from his end. I went out of my way not to hurry things. We would make small talk. On his birthday I gave him one of my books that I thought he would enjoy. (I later found out he hated to read. Good choice, old man.) I had intended nothing more than to act friendly toward him. One Saturday morning as I was leaving with my bag of clean clothes he asked,

"Can I follow you home?"

It seemed to be a strange request – certainly phrased in an unusual way.

"Sure," I came back. "If it's okay with your mother.

But you don't have to follow me. We can walk side by side I suppose."

He smiled understanding the intended humor. His mother approved – we had also become friendly over the weeks I had been going there. We walked home. Wayne kept up a constant line of chatter. It was nice – comfortable, familiar even. He said what was on his mind and asked whatever came into his mind. There were no socialized filters. There was crisp, refreshing, honesty about the boy. He was naive, uncultured, and a grammatical disaster yet his genuineness showed through immediately.

We arrived at my place – about a mile walk.

"You can come in, if you want to, but don't have to, you understand."

"Can I leave the door open?"

"Of course."

Without hesitation he followed me inside and closed the door. We may have had a soda – I don't remember. From that day forward our friendship grew. My reservations about putting him in danger waned. That was probably strictly selfish on my part – irresponsibly selfish, I suppose.

We had virtually nothing in common but found ways of enjoying each others company. We played cards, checkers, and chess – his choices. We worked crossword puzzles – my choice. He caught on fast and his vocabulary grew by leaps and bounds. He confessed to me that he had an attention deficit disorder. It was not news to me but I didn't let on. He was open and honest to a fault. He dropped in almost everyday after school. I helped him with homework. He began taking pride in the improved grades that he learned he could make. I found little jobs for him do for me and paid him. Fourteen year old boys need spending money and I wasn't willing to just fork it over. It was best, I believed, if he felt he was earning it. He was a good worker.

We always laughed when we were together – often uncontrollably. It was fun for both of us. It was useful for both of us. He didn't have many close friends. I didn't have many close friends. One day I realized we were each other's best friends. He looked upon me as a grandfather and I was

70

pleased to have a grandson if only in our fantasy. I should have had other adult friends. He should have other teenage friends. Neither of our situations allowed that at that moment in our lives. It was a healthy – healthful – relationship. We both grew from it.

It was at that time that the late night phone calls began. It had a strange beginning. One morning I awoke to a cold sweat. I remembered that during the night the phone had rung. I got up and answered it. In the past I wouldn't have but now with Wayne in my life I felt some responsibility in case it was he who was calling. Instead, it was a man's deep, raspy, voice.

"Just wanted you to know you can't hide from me. I feel the need to hurt somebody. Not sure who it will be yet – or when."

Twenty-six words that turned my life upside down once again. There was no reason not to believe it was legitimate and tied to the 'crime boy's' family. I was quite sure nobody else had reason to torment me in that way. It had been an odd statement. The best – most responsible – plan would have been to wean Wayne away from me for the sake of his safety. I had no idea how to go about that short of moving again. Wayne was persistent. I had promised the boy my friendship and moving would not be fair to him but then keeping him in what might be harm's way wasn't fair either. It was another dilemma with no good solution. I had been given no timeline. My gut feeling was that the phone call's purpose had been nothing more than to rekindle my terror – something Tony might have decided all those years in relative safety might have tempered. Still, I could not afford to ignore it.

It was a stomach churning conundrum. I had already been living as if the bad guys were out there watching me. This really didn't change that. If anything it should provide relief – from that moment on I knew, without doubt, that my assumption was correct. I was being watched. My safety was vested in their whims. Odd as it may seem, my saving grace in all of that was that I felt sure they would rather see me tortured – mentally and emotionally – than just kill me outright. If I could just accept that, then life could actually

71

become easier. For him to kill Wayne would prevent me from having to worry about his safety. I truly believed the boy was safe.

Every single day I agonized over the loss of my wife and son. I routinely cried myself to sleep over it. (Did you know that a pillowcase, when drenched in tears night after night, becomes stiff?) There was no doubt that although it certainly had not been my intention, it *had* been my laxity with the timeline that had caused their deaths. I suppose that even after having heard the boy recount the atrocities that his family regularly committed, a part of me couldn't believe that human beings could really act in such a vicious and heartless manner. I knew better intellectually but deep down, where I characterized the positive potential of humanity, I had not accepted it. If I did, most everything I stood for, everything I believed about mankind's potential, every hope I had for our future as a species living together in safety, health, and harmony came into question. I supposed that had everything to do with why I had been working overtime to so fervently spread the message of positive social values through my writing.

There were no more calls for several months. Then, occasionally, there would be one. They had changed in nature. The other end remained quiet as if the mere contact was intended to remind me of the message and renew the terror. It worked. My, how it worked. Since they knew I had no way of knowing whether or not they were harming my former patients I doubted if they would risk being found out by actually inflicting harm that way. Did that make Wayne a more likely candidate? It was a new perspective. I shuddered.

I came to believe – to convince myself, perhaps – that he was not in danger. If he were to be harmed I would have no one's safety to worry about and worry seemed to be the bottom-line for Big Tony. Keep the man worried – riled, desperate, fearful, guilt-ridden, terrorized. Ha! Ha! What fun to see the man dance. I hoped that conclusion had not been born from my need for Wayne in my life. He was the focus of my love. He was the one I could do for, care for, and prepare for eventual life on his own. I needed those things. I really needed those things. Certainly it might have been more appropriate coming from adult relationships. Those continued to pose problems.

I had avoided relationships with women for several reasons. I continued to feel some loyalty to my wife. Intellectually I knew that was nonsense but my emotional, guilt-driven, irrationality would not allow me to contemplate another relationship. Also, I couldn't risk putting someone else in danger because of her association with me. Did I long for such a relationship? Almost every day. I needed a woman's companionship, her points of view, her touch. I needed someone who let me attend to her needs (or at least who would let me believe I was doing that). I needed romance. What I needed and what I would allow were polar opposites. I consciously fought against such thoughts. It was a futile effort, much like telling myself not to think of a large, green, elephant riding a bright red scooter.

I continued to work. I continued to write. I continued to spend time with Wayne. I continued to live in fear. It had become a generalized, ever-present, underlying, fear that was just always there, heavy in my stomach. That was in contrast to its earlier version, which was triggered by big men, shadows, darkness, and the red twirling lights of emergency vehicles. Once in a while something would happen, come into view, or pop into my mind that would whip it up into chest heaving, hyperventilating, terror, but that was rare – no more than once or twice a week, perhaps. It sometimes occurred when an unfamiliar vehicle would pull to a stop in front of the business at which I worked – especially early in the morning when I was there alone.

How can I say this in kind and respectful way? Wayne had never actually shaken hands with the King's English. He spoke Ozarkian, which I find delightful, but it caused no small problem for him when it came to written assignments in school. I figured if he got deeply involved in a writing project with me – writing a book for other teens – he might show sufficient interest to work on that. What I found was a wonderfully creative mind with little interest in investigating alternative forms of English! Our first 'conference' about 'his' book was over pizza in a local . . . pizza place. (I am profound!) I asked questions that had to be answered upfront about the basic philosophy he wanted to impart, the story line, the characters and their description, and so on the way most writers prepare. He never missed a beat. I'd ask. He'd answer. When he didn't understand what I was asking he'd grill me until he did. Two hours later we had the makings of a really nice story. It included adventure, romance, excitement, poignant moments, sporting events, humor and tears. It was born of the real life concerns of real life adolescents. I learned a great deal about his life that afternoon.

In the end I did most of the word to the page writing based on his constant flow of ideas and phrases and good questions ("How can we make her seem to really like him without looking that way on her outside?" "I'm not sure. You have some idea, Wayne?" "Well, she could tell her friend who told Suzie who told Joe who told him.") As I'd roll out a chapter Wayne would go over it in great detail. He was a self-professed hater of reading. I'm sure he had never read things with such a critical eye before. ("I don't like the word, *compassion*, there. Kids won't be sure what it means. How about some other word?" Most kids might have actually known, but he didn't realize that.)

In the end we would have a meeting of the minds. Sometimes I required that my experience be the decision maker even if it went against his preference. He never questioned it once I told him how I came upon my decision. A month later *Lucky In Life* rolled off the press with his name first and mine second. It was as much a thrill for me as for him. He showed a copy to his football coach (who bought it, of course) and from then on he referred to Wayne as *Lucky*. The other guys picked it up. It thrilled him. It certainly thrilled me – seeing the positive boost it gave his self-esteem.

Eventually we would collaborate on two more teen novels. He grew in his skill as a writer and his realization that he truly has a creative gift. I grew in my understanding of the current day adolescent mind and socialization process. Wayne was happier with his realizations than I was with mine. Kid's had become so self-centered, so willing to destroy others, so

74

unfeeling about those who were in need or want. Some of that has always been a part of the adolescent years but what I was seeing and hearing was magnified many fold from what I had known before. I shuddered for the future of our society.

I began helping other youngsters with their writing projects and tutored lots of Jr. High age kids in 'translating how they talked into the school version of written English'. The approach was similar to English as a Second Language – written English as a second language for 'English' speaking youngsters. I never put them down for how they had learned to speak. I just provided a system for them to translate it into school-type writing. The added extra was the way *some* changes always followed into their spoken language.

When my wife and I first began taking in foster kids I learned an important lesson. Never change a kid so much that he can't refit himself back into his home and neighborhood. It came to me in flash the day Neal said, "If I talked at the pool hall the way we talk here at your place, I'd be totally rejected – that is, I'd be told to git my high class ass outa there and never show my f'n head inside agin."

I got his point and never fail to think about it when I work with youngsters. I point them toward alternate possibilities but don't undermine what they bring to the table. I suppose that is how all quality relationships progress, isn't it!

On one occasion and with great reluctance I agreed to talk with the son of a friend of a colleague from work. I usually managed to avoid such situations. I hid from such responsibility. He was twelve, in constant trouble outside the home, and was destroying his family and his classroom. His father physically forced him, lock kneed, into my apartment – his large, strong, hands digging deeply into the lad's shoulders. The father left and would be back in an hour. The boy folded his arms across his chest and mounted the world's greatest pout.

"I ain't changin' for you or nobody!"

"Good for you! That's exactly what I like to hear from guys your age."

I got the look.

"You shittin' me?"

"No. I don't do that."

"I don't get you."

The boys pre-planning had been neutralized – 'flushed' he would have said. He found himself afloat. He wrinkled his brow.

"Lot's of guys who come to see me tell me that."

"I'll *bet* they do. You're weird."

"Want to hear what I meant?"

"If you want to tell me."

"It's not about what I want, here. It's all about what you want."

He shrugged his shoulders.

"Okay. I want!"

"I want to help you become exactly the guy you really want to be – forever."

"Honest??"

"Honest!"

"How come?"

"When I was about your age I had some folks help me out – help me figure out what kind of I guy I needed to be if I was going to live a happy life, get girls to like me, hold a job, be successful. So, I try to pass it on when I can. But I never force it on anybody. I only talk with guys who want to talk and listen."

"I suppose I could listen – for just a little while though, maybe, ya see?"

His degree of commitment was overwhelming. From that point on we were able to grow a positive, useful, relationship. His father was amazed as his son headed up the walk on the run when let out of the car in front of my place. I presented the options he would have to face in life and he developed the probable outcomes of each. He began making educated choices. Occasionally he asked for information. We proceeded on the bases that nobody could tell him what choices to make. His success or failure would be his own. There were resources he could use. He had already started down that path by using me. We talked on perhaps a dozen occasions. He won't be president but he won't end up behind bars either. He has a good chance now of being a good son, a

76

good friend, a good boyfriend, and eventually a good husband, father and worker. I'm proud of him. I feel good about myself. His parents, teachers, and neighbors think I am a God. (It's nice to be recognized for what you are!!!)

"How much did my dad pay you to do this?"

It came up during our final conversation that last day.

"Nothing."

"I still don't get you, sometimes. *I* sure as . . . heck can't pay you, you know."

"Oh, but you can."

"What?"

"Someday, when you feel wise enough, you find a boy who needs to talk about life and you do with him what I've done with you. That is how you can pay for this."

"I have a choice in that, you know," he said grinning.

"To pay or not to pay?"

He nodded.

"But for you, now, is it really a choice?"

He grinned again.

"You and your questions. I guess not. How will I know when I'm wise enough?"

"When you no longer have to wonder if you're wise enough?"

That time he nodded *and* grinned.

"Thanks, you know."

"You're welcome, you know."

It was our first and last hug. It was plenty to last me my lifetime.

From time to time there would be others, but I remained doggedly reluctant about the activity. I had, understandably I think, become unwilling to take responsibility for someone else's life. I still had to consider the possibility that I might be putting them in jeopardy. Selfishly, I wanted my time for myself.

Wayne began falling in love – regularly and repeatedly. As his social commitments increased, the amount of time we spent together dropped dramatically. It was how things were supposed to turn out. I could feel good about that. I wrote more. I tutored more. Except for that one thing, life was very,

very, good. I became afraid that the bad guys might 'see' that happening so I decided to take steps to make it less obvious. How they could determine that, I hadn't a clue. About all I could do was wipe the smile off my face when out in public. Again, I became concerned about what steps the 'family' might decide to take and on whom they might take them.

Eventually Wayne graduated, well up in his class. I was proud of him for that. He had applied himself well. Better still, I believe he was proud of himself though that was never stated. Clearly, I have not helped him become a lover of learning the way I had hoped to. He doesn't ask the big questions in life and then go seek the answers. He doesn't take steps to improve his education or his knowledge about the important aspects of life – budgeting, financial planning, interpersonal relations, childrearing, and so on. For that I feel sad. He seems content to be entertained instead of becoming fully engaged in life. However, Wayne is a wonderful human being who is immediately likeable. He can talk with anybody. He likes people and people like him. He takes care of folks. On his own he has become a deeply religious young man. He is a good worker and doesn't shy away from difficult tasks. He is flawlessly dependable. We still enjoy each other's company fairly regularly. I'm intrigued and somewhat amused by the way he now looks out for and takes care of me. How nice.

I have included these several instances to demonstrate how my life, though dread-filled in most ways still had its highlights. Things continued happening that made me feel good and useful and competent above and beyond my newfound skills at dishwashing, dressing salads, and entering an endless stream of mindless information into a database.

As my highs became higher my lows seemed lower – whether they were or not I can't be sure. It became necessary to get increasingly larger and more frequent fixes of positive experiences – positive feedback – to offset the downside of things. It was as if I had an addiction. I had to rein in my needs – control my risky behavior – forgo the highs I had begun seeking, needing, expecting. I went cold turkey.

Things just happened to be at a point where that could

occur naturally. I had no commitments and no outstanding obligations. I went into hibernation, burying myself in writing. I churned out three new Raymond Masters Detective Mysteries in as many months. I liked writing mysteries from a number of standpoints. The good guy always won in my versions. The dead guys were always soooo evil that it eased my conscience about having them rubbed out. Detective Masters presented a positively helpful, cheery countenance. He clearly liked himself and people, and other people liked him. His expertise was obvious – he didn't have to hide his the way I did mine. He clearly had no real concern about his largeness and could and did eat whatever he wanted. I typically gained five pounds while writing one of those books. It was a period of good escape. I got my warm fuzzies from the phrases I framed and the characters I created. Life felt fine. I had reined in my addiction to obvious, public, successes and again found comfort within myself. I liked that self better than the other one.

Still no hint of a name. At one point I began reading phonebooks looking for familiar first and last names. Some I liked better than others but none clung to me.

I remained baffled as to how my name could have been buried so deeply when so much of the rest of my life had surfaced with only a little prodding. What was in my name that my mind needed to keep hidden? That was the wrong question. What would I learn that I couldn't handle if I remembered my name?

There was a chance that the life I had recreated was not accurate in all of its dimensions. It did seem right but there might be nuances that could change things dramatically. What did I really know? So far I had not been unable to verify any but the barest bones of the story. Could there have been other aspects to my crime family connection? I drew a blank. Was there some other problem in my life coincidental to the crime family boy and his situation? Could it have been large enough to send my mind into melt down?

It took me back to the conundrum about the possibility of being a bad guy. I read and re-read case studies of fugue states in which people took on personalities that were quite different – opposite even – from their original. I had to hold it as a possibility – a most unpleasant and disgusting possibility. My stomach still did sink when I spotted policemen. My interpretation was that it related back to the evening I lost my family and policemen were in such perfusion. Perhaps it was something else. I would do some Deep Mind Mastery techniques and see if I couldn't resolve the problem. I was intrigued by why I hadn't considered doing that before. I was so compartmentalized. What I did so readily for others I had not considered doing for myself. Odd. Maybe even bizarre. It seemed some part of me didn't want to delve – didn't want to make those discoveries. That was just so unlike me – the seeker after truth and knowledge.

I needed to catalog my emotional responses. Were there even momentary tinges of negative, destructive emotions that I was not allowing to fully blossom in my new life? Anger? Not really. Revenge? None that I could find. Evil intentions? Certainly not. Unless the villains in my stories were acting them out. That was interesting. But then, my uplifting characters could just as well be acting out my *positive* traits. As *unsettling* as these questions and my non-answers were, it was even more *fascinating*. The human mind was an incredible arrangement of processes and crossroads and deposits of memories and experiences and reaction patterns. No wonder I had spent my life studying it – as a psychologist, as a writer, and now as a mental invalid.

Decades before, there had been a wonderful TV spot aired – I believe, by the Negro College Fund. *A mind is a terrible thing to waste.* A black comedian of the day did a parody of it in his act. At the time it seemed hilarious. Now it seems to hold a basic, unnerving, truth for me. He said: *A mind is a terrible thing. . .* and stopped.

I want to relate, here, my intensive exploration of my Deep Mind. To do so in a meaningful manner I must digress and provide a short *Deep Mind Mastery 101* for the reader. It will be a short version of my model of the mind and how it works. (See *The Secrets of Deep Mind Mastery, 4th ed.*)

The Deep Mind is all about protecting and preserving its person. In many ways it represents the original paranoia in the

80

species. It is cautious to an extreme and resists change when the original idea or behavior seems to be doing fine as is. It leads us to be immediately suspicious of people we don't know and ideas that challenge our status quo – to protect us from possible, as yet unfounded, undefined, harm. Those who refuse to move beyond that first impulse to pull back within the known and safe, live shallow lives, often lives of hate and fear and belligerence. I couldn't let myself slip into such growth inhibiting mental stances.

Very briefly, in my model of the mind ('mind' being those processes that take place within the brain) there are three parts. *The Surface Mind* is that with which we engage and experience the World around us. It is basically verbal and logical in its functions. We are aware of most things going on there. *The Deep Mind*, which is the repository of Directives that often irrationally guide our lives, functions non-verbally, emotionally, and illogically, banking on correlation as the basis for its decision making. (If 'A' occurs just before 'B', then the DM assumes that 'A' caused 'B'. Flick a light switch and the light comes on. In that case correlation seems dependable. Twice when Bobby wears his red sox, his team wins. Therefore the wearing of the red sox caused them to win. I don't think so! – that is, my logical Surface Mind doesn't think so even though I'd be hard put to convince my Deep Mind differently.) The goings on in the DM are generally unknown to us in any direct fashion. We infer them from behaviors, feelings and such things.

In between the Surface Mind and the Deep Mind resides the *Great Filter*. Its job is to only allow information into the DM from the SM that agrees with what is already comforted into the DM. Some new stuff slips in on its own sometimes and there are ways of sending specific new and even contrary items into the DM using certain techniques. But in general the motto of the GF (great filter) is: Don't rock the Deep Mind's boat. (That sounds like the makin's for a Sprirtual! Mahalia, where are you when I need you?)

Bypassing detailed descriptions of the SM and GF functions I want to dwell on the Deep Mind because that seems to be the seat of my turmoil. For sake of illustration, and understanding that the DM really isn't a physical structure that resides anywhere, I anthropomorphize it in this way. Picture a cozy cave deep inside your brain. The temperature is just right. Color its walls and ceiling a comfortable, pleasing hue. There is a wonderfully inviting recliner sitting on a warm, inviting, carpet. The chair faces a wall with hundreds of cubbyholes, like those used at the Post Office for sorting mail. Each is just large enough to hold a small number of 3 X 5 inch cards. Those cards that you see sprinkled around among those little boxes, the cubbyholes, each contain a single Directive. A Directive is a requirement to act or think in a certain way. On the top row of the boxes sits a single, wider, box painted bright red representing life, action, importance, now. It is the card or cards residing in that box that directs the behavior and thinking of the individual at the given moment.

As you observe that wall you see cards floating into and out of that box and rearranging themselves within the other boxes below. It all appears quite willy-nilly. The red box reacts to the activities and thoughts of its person and fills itself with the directives it believes are called for at the moment. It pulls in what it needs and it dispatches those it no longer needs. There is a problem. Most situations that we face have been faced before and so there have already been many, related, situation-specific 'cards' (directives) written in the DM. At any given moment the DM may pull up a fully appropriate directive or it may pull up one that only minimally correlates to the situation at hand.

Let me illustrate: I am approached by a man in a white coat. My stored 'cards' (directives) about white coated guys include experiences from formal dinner parties, the meat packing house, and a doctor's office, among others. Most directives have emotions attached to them. If the emotion attached to the party coat is positive *that* is the feeling that accompanies it to the surface. Should it be terror, then that becomes the associated emotion. If as a child I had a really bad experience in a hospital filled with white-coated doctors I probably still have a directive stored somewhere in my DM that has terror associated with white coats. If, as I enter the 'white coat' dinner party, that 'hospital' card gets sucked into

82

the red box (it isn't particular which 'white coat' card it pulls in – no logic, remember) I may experience a sudden rush of fully unexplained terror.

In my Deep Mind Mastery Program I teach people how to reach down into that complex of boxes and extract and delete unnecessary, hurtful, directives so they can never again cause problems. I also show how to implant more useful directives that can make life simply wonderful. When emotional turmoil exists, it is almost always due to some illogical mess-up in the Deep Mind. That is why it will be the target of my further investigation into the causes of *my* amnesia.

One more set of axioms related to the Deep Mind's method of operation. It has to do with which Directive (card) it will choose to move into the red – action – box at any given moment. *Recency of use* is perhaps the most important reason a Directive gets selected. Once used, a directive is stored in a cubical very close to the red box for ease of future discovery and access. The more recently used it is, the closer it will reside. A second axiom concerns *Emotional Intensity*. When a Directive is 'sent' into the DM with great emotion – positive or negative – it *automatically* gets a seat very close to the red box. A life long behavior pattern (Directive), such as being easy going and kind, can be over ridden in a second when a related directive arrives wrapped in terror or shame. It can cause a personality to change in a moment and continue along that new path so long as the powerfully emotionalized directive remains active in the DM.

So, the Deep Mind is illogical, non-verbal (actually, *poorly* verbal, as it can use minimal language), correlation-based, self-protective above all else, directs ones life based on the directives that get stored there, and decides which directives to engage depending on recency of use, emotional intensity, or mere whim.

The Deep Mind is structured as a question answering machine which, in general, only responds to positive inferences. It doesn't like to be told what to do. It takes negative words such as *don't, never, etc.* and immediately turns them positive – *do, always, etc.* Tell a child not to look

83

in the closet and you can bet he'll be peeking first chance he gets. Don't do drugs??? Well, you get the ideas. When you are trying to change behavior – yours or somebody else's – approach the issue in a positive manner using questions not commands. ("How can I," rather than, "Make me" or "You must!")

Just one more piece of background information. How do Directives come into being in the first place? The DM has the goal of *causing* those behaviors and thoughts it believes the person wants. As life progresses, the person behaves in certain ways, each time sending a directive down to the DM. Although the Filter does its best to cull out pending directives that really don't fit with those already stored, some still slip through. Those attached to high emotion always get through. The DM accepts whatever it receives. It believes the Surface Mind completely and usually without reservation. So, in some instances – *many* over a lifetime – contradictory or competitive directives reside virtually side-by-side in those cubbyholes. The larger the number of dissimilar directives that exist, the more likelihood there is that seemingly contrary behaviors relating to the same topic will be called up from time to time – more erratic behavior patterns will be evidenced. Remember, the Deep Mind uses no logic in calling up a Directive but reacts according to either recency or emotional intensity. When only one applicable Directive is stored, *it* will be called up, of course. If there are several of equal intensity, usually the most recently used will be called up but, this is the illogical, correlation-based, Deep Mind we're talking about. There is often just no apparent rhyme nor reason about how it operates. If I were to coin a motto relating to how we should care for our DM it might be: *A cleaned up deep mind is an efficient, helpful, deep mind.* Get rid of the unwanted, unneeded, hurtful, inappropriate, stuff, and build a base of helpful, happiness, safety producing stuff.

That is essentially what I am building up to with this section – to see if, using these principles, I will be able to help solve the mystery that has its answer mired down in some relatively inaccessible cubby in the far reaches of my Deep Mind. I will not so much be searching for the lost memory as for the directive that requires that memory to remain hidden. If I can locate that and delete it then the memory should be free to surface.   This should be quite a trip – several, most likely.

It is not all positive going into this. I have to assume that if my mind decided to keep the memory from me, it believed that I could not handle it. If that is true – if that is right – and if I unleash it, the result could be disastrous. I believe that I have to try.

CHAPTER FIVE
Exploration

It was to be an unusual application of my Deep Mind Mastery technique so extraordinary planning was necessary. I realized it was not a good fit to the problem at hand but it was all I had. A typical application requires knowing the specific problem and devising a positive alternative to replace it.

For example, a friend of mine had developed panic attacks every time she got behind the wheel of a car when she knew the trip would involve interstate driving. We tracked its origin to riding with her dangerously reckless, alcohol prone, father when she was a small child. Her fear had apparently sat latent in her DM (not in a frequently used cubby and with time-diminished emotional value). Recent reasons to remember about him had dredged up that fear-based association with riding in a car (a directive to be afraid – terrified – when riding the interstate). So, I coached her to construct a collage of images from her past all related to those earlier frightening rides. She infused them with sounds and smells as well as their visual components. She then developed a collage of images and feelings that represented how she wanted things to be. There was music she liked, smiling faces, beautiful byways to enjoy, and complete freedom from anxiety and unnecessary tension. In this way we had the problem images in one collage and the positive replacement solution in the other.

The process was to see and fully experience the negative, reduce it in size, blow it up, and immediately replace it with the positive. Within a half-hour her problem (the panic attacks) were gone forever and driving again became a pleasant activity. She had deleted a negative, disruptive, directive and replaced it with a positive, helpful directive. (Be advised that this has been an oversimplification of the actual, full-blown, process.)

In my case the problem was not so easily defined or pictured. The solution (my name) could not be specified. I had to find some back entrance. The actual problem was having forgotten – not knowing – my name. The positive replacement would be to see my name or hear my name. Since I possessed absolutely none of the necessary information I would have to try some tricks.

In the problem collage I created a set of images in which I would shake hands with people entering my office – the image of the one I earlier reconstructed. I would say, "Hello, Jim, Mary, Bob, Elizabeth or whoever." In return they would say, "Hello, Doctor Blabla." I kept the last name indistinct and muffled so it could not be understood. I imbued it with negative emotions and my unending aggravation about it.

In the replacement collage, I used a similar set of images but left the BlaBla section blank – "Good morning Dr ____." The hope was to trick my mind into supplying it. Again I used the verbalizing and tape recording method to capture the results.

I reclined in my customary comfortable position and did my initial relaxation techniques. I pictured myself sitting in a very comfortable chair in the center of a small, empty, darkened, Movie Theater. On the front of the right arm of the chair was a joystick with a red button handy to my thumb. I created the two collages, which I described above. With the joystick in the rear position I projected the negative collage onto the huge screen across the wall in front of me. I imbued it with fearful emotions, irritation, bright noxious colors, and uncomfortable uncertainty. I examined it for some time

88

letting the feelings of foreboding take hold of me and heighten my terror. Then I pushed the joystick forward. The image on the big screen reduced to the size of a postage stamp – a speck in the center of the screen. I pushed the red button and the image exploded. A whirlwind appeared and sucked its dust up and out of the room carrying it to the four corners of the World so it could never be reassembled. I then immediately eased the stick back toward me and up came the second collage filled with positive, expectant, feelings. It covered the screen. I moved my attention from one of the images to another listening to each greeting, hoping to hear that last name. I had to smile through my great disappointment. Time after time the greeting came through as, "Dr. Blank". I tried it a second time with no better result. I roused myself, prepared to begin formulating plan "B".

That first approach did not appear to have worked although understanding how the mind operates I knew there was some possibility the result might be delayed. (One other characteristic of the Deep Mind is that it never sleeps so when asked a question it may work on it for days before it offers an answer. Ever give up trying to recall a person's name only to have it pop into mind at some later time?)

Next, I would try the, "How can you help me ___" approach. It amounts to a request for help in an indirect way. "How can you help me go to sleep, now?" "How can you help me relax before my speech?" "How can you help keep me from becoming tongue tied when I meet a new girl?"

The most direct question would be, "How can you (meaning my Deep Mind) help me discover my name?" Very likely, it would not be that simple. My *which* name? I had been going by Jerry Wilson for many years. I suspected that was the 'my name' my DM was believing. (Recency) My DM had no ties to the truth of my birth certificate. So, even modifying the question to read, "How can you help me discover my *real* name," would likely not avoid the problem. "How can you help me recall the name I used in college," might be more likely to work or, "How can you help me recall the name I used the day I was married?"

Those might still be too direct considering how hard my

Deep Mind was working to protect me from uncovering it. I would give it a try. If it didn't work there would be Plan C.

I decided to use that last question referencing my wedding day. It held great potential for huge emotion to be tied to it. Again I assumed my comfortable position and again I used my familiar relaxation techniques. I smiled when I discovered my black apple had apparently healed itself of the bite that had been extracted from it. I just *had* to rotate it to make sure. I did and it was. I turned on the recorder and positioned the mike.

"I want to return to the deepest state of focused openness available to me. I am well practiced and an expert at attaining this state so just let it happen. Deeper and deeper relaxed. More and more open. More and more focused. Deep Mind, my good friend, 'How can you help me recall the name I used the day I was married?' "

I lay there in silence, clearing my mind by examining ever nook and cranny of my black apple. Focused attention on some miniscule objective is a preferable technique to trying to maintain a blank mind – which can never be attained. Time passed. I directed the apple to rotate one way and then another consuming my attention on just that one thing, thereby freeing the rest of my mind for the real task. I had it change hues through the rainbow. I examined the stem and the indentation from which it extended. I gave my DM every opportunity to answer my simple question. Nothing came to mind. I gave it more time. It is seldom helpful to repeat a question. The DM seems to get confused thinking it has two separate questions to work on rather than just the one. Still nothing surfaced. I roused and sat up.

Plan 'C". I would simplify the form of the question into a yes/no format by preparing a long list of first names and merely plugging each in turn into the question format, "Was my wedding day first name ____?"

I went through the alphabet – Aaron to Zorba. Again I roused after an hour with nothing to show for my effort. Had I not known and clung to the possibility that my DM was still working on the problem, I would have been terribly disappointed.

Plan 'D'. I would just enter my DM by establishing an open focused non-engaged mind and ask no question. It was like making it guess what it was supposed to do. I had used it successfully with patients who had no idea what in their past might have instilled some terror, anxiety, or phobia. It typically worked well – something better than fifty percent.

Again I relaxed and opened my mind – that time watching the comfortable, blue, mist, engulf me and warm me and soothe me. I floated, weightless in the mist, defocusing my mind from the world and my problems and just experiencing myself there in the mist. I fell asleep, which was fine, usually helpful, even. It was nearly three hours later when I awoke.

Although I felt certain nothing useful had happened, I engaged the voice activated tape recorder just in case and, upon playback, was amused when all I heard was the gentle sound of me snoring. But, there had been something else – something unsettling – a dream – a nightmare; it as hard to characterize. No details awoke with me. Immediately I reengaged my state of relaxation and asked if my DM could reconstruct that dream for me.

That it could and would do. It was as if it had been sent to me as an attempt at communication and was thoroughly peeved that it had to repeat its effort. The surroundings were ill defined – a large interior setting with a lethal injection gurney in a small alcove at one edge of the scene. I was moving from place to place in a big room. It was adorned with old fashioned appointments. I was clearly busying myself with tasks, which I could not specify but which seemed important to me. A large, kindly looking, man followed me around, a Bible in one hand and a syringe in the other. He kept apologizing to me, saying things like, "I'm really sorry to interrupt you, Sir, but the first dose doesn't seem to be working. I need to give you a second injection."

I stopped and held out my arm feeling fully cooperative. My emotion was dutiful compliance with no fear or hesitation. I would then continue doing things. The sequence was repeated numerous times. I would get the shot, do my doings, and then be told I had to receive still another injection. The dream reconstruction had no end. Whether I died or not, or whether it just streamed off into limbo – which I suspect – I really don't know. Then conclusion seemed to be of little consequence. I awoke to the feelings of . . . they are impossible to fully designate. It was a neutral, detached, matter of fact sort of reaction – a mental shrug.

Clearly it represented an attempt to administer a court ordered lethal injection. The gurney with the witness room windows on each side of the little alcove were plainly a part of the picture so it must have been legitimate and not an attempt by the bad guys. The image of a badge on the bible toting big man's chest appeared as I thought about it as if to prove or emphasize the legitimacy.

Was it saying I had done something for which I had accepted the death penalty as legitimate? What horrendous thing could that have been? If there were any truth in it, why had that not come as a part of my life history as I had reconstructed it? Had my mind hid that from me along with my name? My delayed, horrified, reaction to the dream was a thousand times more intense than had been the emotion with which I had awakened. Odd! How could I explain that? Had one of my 'action plans' initiated some riling inside of the DM and allowed that . . . what? . . . impression . . . to surface?

It was a disconcerting element in the matter that has never left me to this day. I didn't want to get rid of it. I could have used the DM collage technique to dispatch it, but I needed to keep it there, examine it, analyze it, and determine what if any truth it held for me. Like I said it was disconcerting and remained there, gnawing at me, just under the surface at all times. It was not debilitating the way my terror had been from time to time but it wore at me. It was the first real indicator I had dredged up from within *me* that indicated that I really could have been a bad guy – apparently a very, very, bad guy! As a dream it didn't ever reappear. As a question it never disappeared.

Plan 'E'. I recorded a word association exercise on a mini-recorder. I listed two hundred words and among them scattered the word 'doctor' a dozen times. In a state of full mental relaxation I started the tape, answering out loud into the microphone.

WORD	RESPONSE
farm	rural
girl	kiss
house	home
doctor	doctor
happy	elated
sad	life
mystery	me
fun	writing
love	family
doctor	doctor
sleep	nightmares
life	difficult
doctor	doctor
name	Jerry
Jerry	Mouse

It went on that way through the list. Although I learned some interesting things about myself, I did not learn my name. It became clear that my original misgiving had proved true. My technique was not intended for the problem I was facing. I was saddened – not because the system had not worked but because, still, my mind could not penetrate the darkness.

I continued to be unwilling to throw in the towel although truthfully I hadn't idea one where to go from there. I remember the sigh of all sighs and a few quick, unexpected, tears – enough to trickle down my cheeks and get lost among the long white whiskers below.

Up to that point – during all those years – I had not really had to struggle against depression. The fear, the constant need to be on alert, the necessity to out think my antagonist, the search for that elusive name, my continued hope that the answers were just around the corner, all kept me passionately in the match. I had always been a problem-solver not a giver-upper. That night, however, as I lay in bed I became concerned about it for the first time. Depression could work to let my guard down, to give up, to become careless and take risks I dared not take. It would be my downfall. I'd likely tell my story in the wrong quarters. I might recklessly decide to go to the authorities and risk everything, not really caring how it all ended. And then there was that ultimate possibility – taking my life. It had been my answer as a teenager. Perhaps it was my built in, bottom line, response.

I was soon asleep – actually *not* a good sign when having those kinds of questions. They should have engaged my mind in a serious and prolonged, pace-the-floor-all-night-in-a-cold-sweat fashion. I should have felt the need to wrestle the night away in an effort to subdue them. Had I already given up? Was I too disheartened to even worry? Depression is the mind's grand defense against overwhelming worry and guilt. Had I finally reached that point?

While I slept that night – unaware of what was happening so unable to muster a defense against it – depression did in fact begin working its numbing fingers into every corner of my mind. The next morning I slept in later than usual. I cut short what in my mind soon became an arduous shower. I omitted the washing of my hair. I skipped my walk and breakfast. I arrived at work twenty minutes late. No one would know since I was there from seven until nine by myself. I would make it up later on. Once there, it became difficult to get down to work. I had invoices to check, phone messages to prepare for answering, and problems from the day before to work out but for the first time I didn't care if it all got finished or not. Such behaviors would have usually concerned me deeply. That morning I swiveled away from the front door and slipped into a nap there in my chair.

The problem with depression is that although you know things are way out of kilter and life is braking to an unexplainable and inappropriate halt, you can't muster the strength to do anything about it. You can't refuel the furnace. You choose to remain seated when you know you should stand. You just watch the hands on the clock click past the time you need to leave or be somewhere. You opt not to respond to advances or inquiries from others. You even wait longer than you should to move to the bathroom. You choose not to dress because of the effort involved. For the same reason you don't eat – or your senses may be so dulled that

94

you may not be aware of an appetite. Everything comes wrapped in a shroud of futility. Virtually nothing has the power to stir you into action. Unfortunately, as the Deep Mind senses that you want to remain in that state, it does its best to facilitate the mood, the feelings, the despair. It becomes a self-fulfilling state of mind.

It was as if my mind was going on vacation right there in the hubbub of my work and responsibilities. A part of me did struggle against it in public. I was a strong person. I had never been one to visit my tribulations on others. I did my best to spare them. I'm sure my sudden quietness and lack of humorous comments tipped everybody off that something was awry. When questioned I would feign headaches or flu or a sleepless night or some other minor malady.

I wanted to stay home but somehow forced myself to go to work. I needed the money for survival, although the worth of that, too, had become dubious. There was at that time a major change in the way commissions were figured at work and my financial health took a terrible turn. I had made financial commitments to help several struggling families in the communities and I did not dare fail to come through for them. That may have been my positive link to sanity. I took a second job – overnight stocking job at a local grocery – to help make up the difference. It was a middle of the night, one mile walk to and from through a deserted area of the city and across a park. The walk became terrifying. The shadows became my nemesis. The noises became ominous, garbled, messages I could not decipher.

Looking back I am impressed with how my strength of character and sense of responsibility to others did not waver through all of that. I did go to work. I did my work. I met my financial obligations to the families. Eventually, it would add to my certainty that I could never have really been the bad guy in whatever had triggered the terrible turn in my life.

Over the next nine months my depression fluctuated between severe and moderate. If anybody was really concerned about me, no one voiced it to me. Either I was a good actor even through my depression or they were less caring than I had believed. Either way is of no real

95

significance. Things are as they are and I don't tend to point the finger of blame. People become absorbed in their own lives and that focus understandably allows many outside things to pass unnoticed. I would have seen their concern as bothersome meddling anyway. It would have added to my problems.

I told Wayne I was having a sever bout of allergies that sapped my energy. He bought it and became even more helpful. It bothered me that I would lie to him in that way but it was another of those unsolvable dilemmas – there was no good alternative. If the truth ever surfaced he would understand and not hold ill will toward me for it. He was a good hearted young man who allowed love to conquer malevolent feelings.

I remember on one occasion standing on a bridge over a tiny trickling stream. Had it been a hundred feet to the rocks below rather then ten I might have jumped. I remember sitting on my couch eyeing the rat poison sitting in its yellow and brown, triangular box near the baseboard on the floor across the room, wondering how long it would take me to bleed to death internally if I were to consume it. Would it hurt? Would it be a messy clean-up for those who found my body? I remember thinking about the box of rifle ammo I had discovered in a closet when I first moved into my apartment and wondering briefly how, without a gun, a bullet might be discharged, aimed at my chest or head. I remember standing in the shower thinking how easy it would be to fill the tub, submerge my body, and drop an operating hair dryer into it.

Knowing that I could so easily take my life and realizing that I had not, started me on the road back out of the depression. I was amazed at how rapidly my mood returned to nearly normal. I walked regularly again and immediately felt better physically. I took time to prepare good meals rather than opening sacks of chips or donuts, or pealing back wrappers on candy bars. I enjoyed being clean and neat. Those things which had been cause for compounding my depression – having to be those ways when I didn't want to be – were no longer a struggle. Most oddly of all, I seemed to welcome the return of the terrors. They confirmed I was alive and waging my best effort against the darkness.

During the worst of those months I had fallen into the fair vs. unfair mind set. Everything about my life was unfair. That way of thinking, of course, can only come about when you see your 'fate' as being determined from the outside rather than from within yourself. It means you take no responsibility for your own destiny but require – allow – outside forces to take care of you. I had never been that way before – well, except during those several months of ultimate distress when I was sixteen. Later it would be nearly impossible for me to imagine having let that happen. I did let it happen, didn't I?

I returned to writing and moved directly into some very heavy pieces – novels – four hundred page tomes that presented my personal philosophy eye to eye with its major challengers. It became a trilogy – the David Lawrence Trilogy (*The Box, The Map, The Strap*). Each required a good deal of research. I welcomed the challenge and basked in the new knowledge. Each required intricate and precise plotting – something my usual pieces really didn't. The five months spent on those three books were exhilarating beyond anything I could remember ever having experienced. I remember thinking that if I should die at that moment I had at least set down my complete social and personal philosophy and my best considered solutions for mankind's major problems – for others to use or ignore as they chose. In the least, I hoped it would demand serious reconsideration of positions, thoughtlessly accepted by the hoards as the truth.

I followed those with two lighter pieces, *How to Be Deep Down Forever Happy* and a novel, which illustrated the axioms of that book, *Ripples*. Ripples turned out to be one of my very favorites of all those I had churned out during the previous fifteen or however many years.

This would be my next book, but I get ahead of the story – way ahead of the story.

The occasional late night phone calls continued. Except in that first one, no words were ever spoken. None were needed to keep the flames of terror burning inside me. Each became a reminder of my status – a helpless pawn whose life

97

or death would be determined at the whim of an evil group of men. Each followed an identical pattern. The phone would ring. I would pick up and say, "Hello". The silence on the other end would last one minute and then the disconnecting click and the dial tone. If I hung up first there would be additional calls until I allowed the sixty seconds and 'his' hang up, first. Nothing was everything. He understood a great deal about the human psyche. Nothing he could say or threaten, no emotion he could impart, would be as terrifying as what I would create – recreate – in my own mind.

Since their outset I harbored a strange feeling about them. They floated somewhere between the real and the imagined. It is hard to explain. I have no 'real' memory of that first call. I mean it was not until the next morning when I awoke that it first appears in my memory. I awoke and then remembered it. There was some subtle difference – some subtle irregularity – that I couldn't put my finger on. It had been akin to waking up and remembering a dream. Could I have dreamed the phone call and the gravely voice and the threatening message? I could have but then how would I account for the subsequent calls? Either all the calls were real or all the calls were dreams. How could I ever know for sure? It was a new way of conceptualizing the situation. I would have to give the possible alternatives careful consideration. The next time I received a late night call I would record the event. I'd record the final ring before I picked up. I would record my answer. I would hold the microphone to the receiver and record the minute of silence, the click, and the dial tone. That should verify the reality of the calls.

Each night for months to follow I set up the tape recorder beside the phone. It seemed the next call would never come. How odd that I *wanted* to receive another call.

I took on several 'ghostwriting' assignments, which brought an influx of funds into my savings. It was about equal to the amount I gave away each month. That seemed to be my compulsive passion – sharing what I had. Still, I tended to obsess about growing that account. At best it would never be more than small but I figured 'big small' was bound to be better than 'small small'. I continued to fret over funding my retirement years. My Jerry Wilson identity would not allow me to receive social security and I had no other sources of retirement income. I was counting on my book sales and ghosting but what if my health took a bad turn and I could no longer write? It became a concern almost equal to any of the others with which I had to deal. I had no insurance – early on it had been too expensive. Now I was past the age for which policies were written. Life, even without the original Tony terror, had become frightening in and of itself.

If I could just find someplace that would let me work for them and they, in turn, would agree to let me live out my years with them. An Inn, perhaps, where I could hold writing seminars, sell my books, make and sell nick-knacks, even work as a janitor or run the gift shop. Perhaps a children's home where I could live-in and do whatever my talents allowed. Find a rich old widow who would support me in return for my companionship and the comforts I could supply. I doubted if I even remembered how to go about the process of providing that kind of 'comfort' any more.

That brought back memories of my wife and our life together. I was finally able to mostly focus in on the good times and overlook the sadness attached to her loss. For the first time it stirred romantic feelings that had lain essentially dormant since the time of her death. I didn't know what to do with them. It took me back to being a twelve year old – feelings with no knowledge of how to tend to them. There would be no big boys to set me on course this time. I felt awkward and alone. I felt sad and unfulfilled. I felt like crying, so I did.

I was or had been a psychologist. Why did I not pursue formal therapy to help me resolve my several dilemmas? Soon after arriving in Joplin I had gone to the local mental health clinic for a session with a young social worker. She insisted that I submit my data to the National Missing Persons Registry. That was her inexperienced answer for helping me. She refused to hear my hesitancy. True, I had not shared any of the scary side of my situation with her, but I had expected some suggestions for attacking the amnesia, therapeutically. She offered none. That was before I had established in my

99

own mind that I had been a therapist. I gave her very low marks and never returned. If a therapist were to be given an honest shot at helping me it was clear I would need to reveal things that I felt I could not reveal. I simply could not risk that, then. I wondered if I could, now. I had no answer.

Uncertainty began to grow. The reality or fantasy of the phone calls – other things.

One morning while I was having my biscuit, grape jelly, and coffee at Rick's Café, half way through my morning walk, I overheard a couple of men talking in the next booth. It had been the word, *Joplin*, that had turned my ear in their direction.

"It wouldn't be a half bad little city if it just had public transportation."

But it did! I had used the bus to get to the Sears store. I saw it all in my mind's eye. The walk down the hill from my place to the bus stop. Depositing my dollar. Taking my seat by the window and checking to make sure the 'chain' was within easy reach.

But wait! My apartment – the garage apartment – sat on level ground with no hill for blocks. There was a fleeting mental glimpse of the house from which I had emerged. It was unfamiliar. It was not the motel or the roach house or the garage apartment from Joplin. It was a small two-story house with two front doors and a porch that spanned the front. There were steps leading up to it. From where had that image come? The mystery of how that memory surfaced was not the source of my suddenly growing terror; it was the confusion, the uncertainty, the possible initial chink in the story of my current life – one that that might signal its imminent collapse.

Surely my memory of those years since finding myself in Joplin was still intact – wasn't it? That had been my rock, my mainstay, my only real certainty but now it, too, seemed to be in question. What was happening? Terror mounted terror. Was I in fact losing my mind?

Looking back, there was some humor and irony in the next inconsistency but it didn't really work to quell my uneasy uncertainty at the time. In an unexplained flash I saw myself in the image I had created of me shaking hands and greeting

100

people at my office. I was wearing a full, nearly white, beard. I arrived in Joplin clean-shaven and wondered, at that time, if I should grow a beard to disguise myself. Five years later I did. The safe harbor that had provided vanished in an instant. Should I shave it again?

If the phone calls were real, my whereabouts were known, beard or no beard. It then became a choice of personal preference. I liked it – scraggliness and all. If the calls were fantasy and if I were still well hidden, then it might make a difference – but only if the 'crime family' was actively searching for me. My terror was overridden by panic. A choice was presented – perhaps a life and death choice for me or other innocents. It had no clearly correct alternative.

I would feel exposed, naked, without the beard. It might, in fact, be the better choice to shave, but that thought increased my panic. From panic would follow confusion and poor decision-making. I had to minimize panic. I had to keep my mind on track, thinking straight. I would keep the beard and live with the uneasy possibility it could be the key to being recognized.

Had the city bus-riding been a dream – an illusion, a delusion? I had the Cricket Stories so the cards from the word processor were probably real – my reason for taking the bus to Sears. I should still have them somewhere. My early floppies were in a shoebox. I would merely open it and find them. I located it. I opened it. I didn't find them. Of course, knowing I could not use them and having their contents printed as hard copy, it would have made sense to just toss them out. Perhaps I got rid of them as I prepared to move to Fayetteville. That made sense – intellectually. My gut fought that attempt at logical closure. Perhaps I had been robbed. Perhaps the family had dispatched somebody to rifle my things either to determine what I was doing or to further terrorize me. I had to consider the possibility that there had never been any memory cards – that I had written the stories early on in my Joplin experience or that the hard copy had accompanied me from wherever.

Things were falling apart. Correction. Things *might* be falling apart. Not knowing which was troublesome. That was too mild a descriptor but 'terror' and its derivatives had become old hat; they had lost their full impact. There had been wonderful advantages to having been depressed. The fact that my life – my mind – might be falling apart would have been of little consequence to me back then had I even recognized it.

The importance of my next decision would be monumental. It would determine my future – life or death most likely. Should I continue the struggle to hold onto sanity or give in to the imagined comfort of collapse? In collapse there would be no more struggle, no more responsibility, no more coping with uncertainty or unhappy memories. There would be no more searching for answers that would not come, no more struggling to find the light there in the darkness of my mind. There would be no more concern about living or dying – my life was no longer really living. That alternative came unencumbered with affect.

To fight would represent a closer fit to the person I had learned I had been – was. It would require inner strength, which I had certainly already proved was mine. It would be unselfish, for in coming to the final, sane, conclusion about it all I would probably be protecting other guiltless, potential, victims. In collapse I would give up self-esteem. In accepting the fight I would endeavor to maintain and even build my self-esteem.

It was my next question, actually, that provided my answer and adjusted my course. It followed a closed eyes deep breath and a bone quaking shudder. I opened my eyes.

"So, what do I need to do in order to endure this period of mind-numbing, suddenly increased, uncertainty?"

The answer suddenly seemed so simple.

"Maintain my routine, listen for new information that verifies, questions or dismisses my current understanding of the situation, and remember that I have survived with some degree of helpfulness and enjoyment those hard years just past. I *did* have a life right there, right then."

I remembered a phrase I was sure I had frequently passed on to my patients: "A life without problems to solve allows for no growth."

102

If that were true I could look forward to a mountain of growth just ahead. It suddenly seemed exciting. My mood was fluctuating wildly. That in itself was seriously discomforting.

I shifted into 'watch and learn' mode. I paid less attention to my terror and confusion as I searched out new nuances to my 'old' memories, my old certainties. I told myself that my Deep Mind was doing some housecleaning – sending me any alternatives that may have been left sitting in their less accessible cubbyholes. It was providing me with new information to search and examine and see if I could find a reasonable fit. I would look upon the situation not as confusion but as the opportunity to mindfully sort through possible alternatives.

The many sterile sorties into my Deep Mind had apparently not been for naught. The results were not what I had expected or requested but apparently represented the answers that made sense to my DM. I needed to be patient and receive the information as it came and use it as puzzle pieces much like when operating without the picture of the finished puzzle. As a child I almost always approached my 'jigs' in that fashion. I loved the challenge at that moment, even while despising the uncertainty, without which, I understood, there would be no challenge.

Assuming that new stance, 'was easier said than done' – isn't that the saying? Apprehension remained. That was undoubtedly a reasonable reaction. I needed to institute a major modification in my approach to thinking about life. What I had been assuming was an absolutely accurate reconstruction of my pre-Joplin days, clearly had some flaws. How many or how devastating to the overall story I had no way of knowing. I wondered why it had taken so many years to surface. That story had been my strength through it all. Perhaps that was the answer. I needed an unwavering base from which to go on. I needed something to believe in. I needed an unshakable identity from which I could move forward. Perhaps my Deep Mind was sensing a new strength I had not yet discovered. It probably made no real difference. Regardless, I had to handle the discrepancies that were amassing and move on. I had to expect and even welcome more modifications. I had to proceed with strength through the uncertainty. After all it was the truth I was after.

I didn't like the new arrangement. I didn't like the new layer of discomfort. I didn't like the idea that the me I had discovered and so easily accepted might not resemble the me of my 'real' past. I was intrigued by how it still seemed so right – how it was so comfortable. Perhaps I had been confusing 'right' with 'comfortable'. Perhaps most of the changes had now been made. Perhaps the basic rendering of my early life *was* accurate. Actually, my concern was as much about the life I thought I had been living since arriving in Joplin as the life before. More, even. There seemed to be a disconnect between the two. It was hard to explain.

I suspected the line between what had been real and what had been fantasy – dreams, wish fulfillment, whatever – had become blurred in certain instances. For one, I imagined that the walk down the hill to the bus had been a dream sequence that had bridged the gap from realm to realm. Certainly I would not have clouded another *actual* home out of my consciousness – would I? If taken at face value, that sequence clearly indicated another city – another, still secreted, period in my history. It had to be some kind of fantasy. It was so difficult to just wait and see how things would eventually fall together. I wasn't used to approaching problems by doing nothing. It was contrary to my every inclination.

Perhaps I needed to occupy myself in some all-consuming way while I waited. There was a new mystery novel I had been contemplating – *The Case of Too Many Suspects* with Raymond Masters. It was a concept piece with a half dozen people admitting to a murder with solid evidence pointing to each of them. I added an old fashioned six-shooter, which was always loaded with blanks, as the murder weapon. What fun it would be to craft. I had a good time. It provided a month of fairly intense diversion.

Virtually nothing happened on the mental front during that time. I wanted to think that was because there was nothing left to happen. It was a dangerous way to be thinking. I had to remain prepared to have my house – if made of cards

– come tumbling down. I assembled a tough attitude about it – cynical and fatalistic to some extent. *Que sara sara.* What happened, happened. It was how thing usually were, but in this instance, under such intense scrutiny, it seemed to be more.

I began having dreams about my childhood – each one pleasant and each one verifying the picture I had previously discovered (or developed). Some were from my early years. Others were from later. They arrived in random sequence. Were they verifying my previous impression? Were they being generated falsely to add credence to my previous impressions to hold at bay any discrepancies and protect that story – my belief? I had no way of knowing. If they were not representative of the truth, they were first class forgeries.

It struck me that I had no recollection of ever having had a dream about myself – about my Joplin and post-Joplin self. Odd, I thought. It had been more than a dozen years. Surely there must have been something dream-worthy in all that time. Then the makings for an interesting science fiction story hit me. What if that day – the day I was experiencing at that moment – was the *first* day of my 'new life? That all of my memories about the years since Joplin were some sort of instant fantasy or delusion. What if there had actually been no dozen years since I left someplace. What if it had been last evening or even this morning – five minutes ago, perhaps?

I looked around as if expecting to see things familiar from my past – my pre-Joplin days. Nothing. Interesting. If I didn't lose my mind first, I'd have to whip that impression into a story someday.

Three aspects of my Manchester connection continued to bother me. First, of course, was the fact the little town just didn't exist. Second and third, that if I had mis-remembered its size and it really had been North Manchester, and if that is where I lived my life, it would have been a 175 mile one way trip from south Chicago – a really long way for the crime family kid to have traveled every week to see me. Perhaps they flew into a local airport and just took the limo to my office. I didn't recall anything along those lines. I would have thought flying would have been novel enough for him to

105

mention. Maybe he flew everywhere so it wouldn't have been special. Why would they have come that distance to have *me* work with the lad when Chicago was thick with therapists? To keep the process anonymous? Because I was the best? Doubtful. Because I appeared to be a first class patsy? Heck, maybe there was no crime family kid so the inconsistencies were irrelevant. I shook my head hard. It was akin to having thumped on my temple that first day in Joplin. Shaking didn't work either.

I had once written a short story about a boy who hated his terrible life and loved his dreams. In the end he discovered that it was his dream life that was real so he no longer had to deal with the unpleasant, frightening, 'other' life. Could it be that I was reliving that plot? Perhaps I was still, really, that sixteen year old back in that small town living out a wonder-filled life among a community of people who loved me and whom I loved. This was just an unpleasant, momentary, nighttime, reverie caused by my overindulgence in Mr. Kohley's bratwurst at the Sunday School picnic. It might account for the lack of dreams about Joplin and after, because Joplin and after would have been a dream itself.

How nice that scenario would be. All I had to do was wake up and life would be wonderful. I didn't understand why I lingered over such absurdities. Wish fulfillment fantasies would not help and might even prolong my 'recovery'. I would need to make a conscious effort to nip each one in the bud from that moment forward.

It was that evening – summer, still hot at eight o'clock – that I decided to walk down to the park and enjoy the coolness that usually hung there between the thick carpet of verdant grass and the deeply bowing branches of the big old maples. Something about the meteorological physics of the spot caused a gentle, continuous, circulation of the air. I took a seat on a bench and opened my shirt to the coolness. I considered but stopped short of removing it. The situation took me back to tales of my early childhood – earlier than I could remember. The story was that daily, during the summer, I would be brought home to Mom, me – naked as a jaybird – under one arm of a strong man and my clothes gathered under

106

the other. I still dislike clothing – it restricts easy motion, drags its coarse surface across my skin, keeps me unpleasantly hot in the summer, and after one or two day's use must be laundered adding to the expenses of life. The needing-to-be-clothed concept seemed absurd but the prudes of my country had clearly won on that score so, when in public at least, I bowed to their power (not to be confused with their wisdom).

It was nearly ten when I decided to begin the trek home. I set a leisurely pace north on the sidewalk.   A set of headlights approached me. I could make out little more than that there in the waning twilight. Closer, I could see it was a shiny, black car. Even closer, I made it out to be a limousine. It slowed and stopped beside me. I figured they had become lost on their way to a party. Limos had no reason to be cruising the darkened park. The rear window rolled down. It seemed to take an eternity. A light went on inside. I saw him. It had to be Big Tony. His well-tanned, chubby, drooping, jowls were highlighted in just a hint of rosy red. His face wore a permanent scowl topped by a deeply furrowed forehead. His eyes sat as slits above his cheeks, recessed below his heavy brow. Not a strand of his regularly died black hair was out of place. A dank, coolness, rushed out to meet me.

I pulled back from my initial, bent at the waist position, which I had assumed while awaiting the expected question for directions. The man removed his half shaft of a cigar and looked me up and down. It was far from the up and down Candy had once given me. It was cold and calculating, inquisitive and yet uncaring. It was James Cagney, Jack Palance, Edward G Robinson, and all the bad guys of old captured in a single take.

I waited for him to speak. I wanted him to speak. He just stared for the longest of moments, then, flicked his gaze directly up into my face. We held each other's eyes for several seconds – it seemed an hour. With our eyes still engaged he stuffed his cigar back into his mouth. The window rolled up, sinister in its slow silence, until his face was gone. The vehicle moved on. He had not uttered a word. He hadn't so much as offered a grunt or a sigh. I don't recall seeing or

107

hearing him breath. He didn't blink. Neither had I. Part of me had wanted to scream at him and place my fingers to his throat and drain the life from his body. Thankfully the more rational part of me disallowed those reactions. I had met him cool for cool. Silent for silent. Steely, squinted eyes to steely, squinted, eyes. Of course I wasn't his match. I knew that. He knew that. It would not be I who would first give hint of it, however.

My courageous front faded fantastically fast. I hadn't realized that knees actually knocked outside of fairy tales. I tried to swallow but the dryness of my mouth and throat did not allow it. I turned just enough to follow the limo out of sight. It was not coming back. Still as I hurried home I stole frequent, quick glances over my shoulder. I paused well ahead of each intersection scanning both directions for sight of the car. My crossing was hurried and awkward as I turned this way and that and peered both down the street from which I had come and up the street, which I was about to enter.

I feared my weary legs were not going to manage the six steps up to my front door. I fumbled for my key. I fumbled *with* my key. I fumbled to turn the knob and enter my living room. The door was quickly locked. I chose to sit there in darkness – quite the opposite from what had given me a sense of security in the past. I took note of the inconsistency but made no move to alter the setting. From end to end my body was quivering, uncontrollably. I was breathing hard, whether out of my terror or from the rapid movement home I could not be sure. Of course I could – it was both!

Eventually, I undressed and went to bed. There was some sense of safety in that. I slept on a pull out couch-bed, which, when unfolded spread within a few inches of the door. With my bed in place the door simply could not be opened. It was a false sense of security but most nights I'd take any sense I could get. That night was *certainly* no exception.

CHAPTER SIX

The Familiar Smell of Diesel
The Familiar Dampness of my Pillow

My mind was clearly still blocking important pieces of my past. What really gave me good reason to believe that any of what it had revealed to me was anything other than a contrived sham? What verifiable tidbits did I really have? Manchester College. I did know things about it. My memory seemed to indicate my involvement in the school paper. That had to be in the 'maybe' column – having no way of verifying that. The College at Geneseo, New York. I knew about it before I found it so I did have some memory of it. None of the rest of the Geneseo memories could I verify, I suppose. They'd go in the 'maybe' column as well.

Joplin. In my mind's eye I could see places – the three places where I lived, the restaurant where I worked, the house in which Sal and his family lived, the bus station, the IGA, the planted area behind the bank. The airport! That was something new. Why would I have been at the airport?

I needed verification of my life in Joplin. I needed to know that *it*, at least, had not been an illusion – delusion. I arranged a roundtrip bus ticket for that very Saturday. With my presence in Joplin imminent, a few other pieces floated into focus. There was another small café that I had frequented somewhere. I believed it was in Joplin. It was set on a lazy street and was surrounded by wonderful old trees and flowering bushes. It looked to have been a garage at one time – long and narrow with windows across the front replacing the wide door. Pancakes. Conversation. Lots of familiar, though nameless, faces. It was most likely a regular, early morning, haunt. I saw me installing my air conditioner in the apartment over the garage. The outlet had been 240 volts and I had to 'fix' it there at the wall and in the fuse box down stairs so it would deliver the 120 my unit needed. I did that without hesitation. What might that tell me about myself? I saw numerous people visiting in my apartment. There was a teen-age boy with a wonderfully full head of hair who was worried about becoming bald. I taught him how to fix his worry. There was another teenage boy who had legitimately-based, deep, issues about women and they were tearing apart his relationship with the girl he loved. I taught him how to fix his problem. There were others – smokers, fighters, patsies, school failures.

Interestingly, the more *that* came into focus the more uneasy I became. It may have represented anxiety related to responsibilities – something I had specifically arranged my life in Fayetteville to avoid.

The Saturday morning arrived. I found I had become an excuse making machine – churning out reasons I should not make that trip. I might be recognized (I was wearing a beard). I might meet people who recognized my voice (I didn't have to talk.) It went on and on. I boarded the bus. Its smell; its low, subtly undulating, rumble; the people; the essential soul of the setting were all familiar – more familiar than I would imagine one or two trips would have engendered. Perhaps that would be important. Had I once been a bus-riding vagabond?

The closer I came to Joplin the more anxious I became. I squirmed. The woman across the aisle seemed to be convinced I needed the restroom. She would hitch her head toward the rear of the bus. 'Joplin 10 miles', read the crisp white letters against the soft green background. Up until that moment the panic within me had been contained to a taut chest, barely noticeable except upon taking an oversized breath. Taut soon morphed into a biting tension as it seeped

110

deeper and deeper into my body. As I remembered it all, I had experienced the same fear during the first few moments after I made my arrival there; "I must not hyperventilate and faint . . ."

It was clearly a monumental event. I had not expected that. After navigating the main thoroughfares and lumbering through the back streets we entered the depot and pulled to a stop in the stall nearest the waiting room. My eye was immediately taken by lock box number 104. I thought that should provide some relief – there it was, proof from the git-go that my 'memories' had some basis in reality. It didn't.

I figured I would need a minimum of four hours to make the places I wanted to verify. I had six until the return trip would begin. I headed south on the same sidewalk I would have taken that first day. I noted the rest area just ahead and stopped, figuring the concrete beneath my feet represented the spot on which I had emerged into my new life. There were no particular feelings attached to it. I couldn't remember having stood there since, and wondered why I hadn't revisited the spot. I moved on and took a seat on the bench. The noonday sun had warmed the cool October air. That day it felt good. I removed my jacket. I could eat but was reluctant to visit any of the café's I remembered.

I walked the block east toward the main north-south street. It was the side-street with the first small café in which I'd eaten. It was still there. I walked on past it, glancing inside, thinking I might come back if it felt okay. I had no feeling so decided that was as good as an okay. I slowed as I approached the main drag. Diagonally to my left would be *Sal's Italian Restauranate*. I stopped to survey the familiar green awning. The restaurant was gone. My heart sank. I knew things had not been going well financially at the time I left. Perhaps it had moved to a better location. I remembered something about that as a possibility. I hoped that was the case. Perhaps it had never been there.

I returned to the smaller café and entered. I lingered over the BLT and fixin's longer than necessary. The panic had subsided noticeably but part of me was still reluctant to pursue the course I had set for myself that day. By my seventh coffee refill my eyelids were incapable of blinking let

111

alone closing. I paid my bill and left, shading the sun from my unsquintable eyes. I moved west past 'my' bench toward the old motel. I knew the route well. Three blocks west and one south – to the left.

Perhaps I *didn't* know the route so well. I stopped and looked across the street where the motel should have been. It wasn't there. It could never have been there on that big lot occupied by a huge old Victorian house surrounded by hundred year old oaks, maples, and pines.

I looked up and down the street puzzled beyond belief. There was a boy on a bike. I flagged him down. He was fourteen or so and seemed willing to interrupt his day for me.

"Is there a motel – old, white, stucco – around here somewhere?'

"No, Sir. Nowhere around here. I've been doing this part of town on my bike for ten years and I can tell you for sure they ain't no motel nowhere around here."

"I guess I was given poor information, then. Thanks for your help and have a great day."

He gave recognition to my rather trite comment with a short, head bobbing, nod and was immediately off down the street. It looked like I was batting, what . . . .750 I supposed – the lock box (yes), the bench (yes), the restaurants (yes), the motel (no). I couldn't understand or explain it but I moved on west to where the old roach house should be. As I neared the location I saw the IGA straight ahead on the right, exactly where it should have been. My spirits soared in anticipation. I turned south. The house should be the second one on the left. There it was! I found myself nodding. My stats were improving. I looked the old house over carefully. The front door to 'my' apartment had been changed; it needed changing. The hinges on the old one were on the outside so it opened out. Anybody with a flat blade screwdriver could have quickly gained entrance. The porch light I had installed and the huge mailbox I had built were still there.

The garage apartment was still further south and then several blocks east. I had traveled it twice a week to and from the IGA for all that time in Joplin. I retraced the familiar steps. I even anticipated the big stone house on the right with

112

the iron fence and the several dogs chomping at the bit behind it. I was sad at the realization that the oldest one – a plump old Boxer – was no longer there. He and I had an unspoken understanding not to unnecessarily expend energy, something the younger pups had not yet learned.

I found the alley that led to the garage above which had been my apartment. It, too, was exactly where it should be. I walked the alley and circled around to look at the house in front. It should have been on Byers Street – that had come to me during the bus ride. It was the house. It was Byers. My feeling about the place was mostly warm and comfortable. I felt much of the extra, Joplin-specific, anxiety drain away.

I was ready to move on. My plan had been to walk to within sight of Sal's home. It was a long walk – nearly twenty blocks north as I recalled. Something pulled me in the opposite direction. I felt like an iron filing being sought out by a horseshoe magnet in a fifth grade science experiment. I would follow the inclination south. As it turned out it was four blocks south and one west. There it stood, the small café with the glass front and the trees and bushes. I was again filled with comforting warmth. I needed to enter. It was going on two o'clock. I'd get coffee (my eyelids screamed at me!) Check that. I'd get a decaffeinated soft drink and perhaps some chips or fries. I needed to use the restroom.

Inside I feigned laryngitis and pointed to cut short the ordering process and associated chitchat, not daring to risk having my voice recognized in case the same folks were there who had been there all those years before. It was a seat yourself place and I was drawn to a table in the front on the left from where I could see outside to the trees and houses across the street. It was a Rockwellian scene. I figured I had to be close to .999 by then and relaxed even more. I looked over the menu as I sipped at the cola and nipped at the chips. They had named various dishes after people – regular patrons I assumed. There in all its glory on the breakfast side of the single, laminated, green sheet was, *Jerry's Short Stack and Sausage*. I fluffed my beard hoping to increase its value as a disguise. It could have been some other Jerry, of course, but I'd choose to think that it referred to me. I had been the center

113

of the universe for so long it only seemed right!

It was as I left the café that I took note of the emotional contrast between it and Sal's – well, where, I believed, Sal's had been. The calm and peacefulness I had just felt stood in severe contrast with what had drifted across the street to meet me from the Italian connection. There, it had been a heavy distress, an anxious presence, a restless uneasiness. I felt an immediate sadness about that because I had loved the people there so very much.

I did determine that there was no public bus system within Joplin. That meant the house-leaving and bus-riding image had to be of another time and place. The phone book verified that there was a Sears store at which, back then, I could have checked out the memory cards but I would have had to have taken a cab. Since Joplin is where my new life seemed to have begun I would assume that was where I visited Sears. (I fully understood that could not be verified unless the smiley little rotund, cheek pinching, supervisor might still be there and remember me! It had been offered as an attempt at humor. Perhaps it actually might have held some validity.) I checked my watch. There would not be time for that trip. I had verified so much that I no longer had any lingering – gnawing – reservations about the reality of the Joplin era in my life. I could not account for the disappearing motel. Why would my mind have created it? Could it have been real but just somewhere else? Perhaps at my stop just before Joplin if there had been a stop – the house, hill, and bus place?

The ride home carried with it a bubbling cauldron of emotions. The positive part of that was that each one seemed to be attached to something – none of the free-floating variety. Those were always the most frightening kind. When police cars scared me at least I knew *what* scared me – I knew the source of the problem, even if only its surface representation. I had a starting place. When I was scared for no apparent reason, I had no starting place, nothing to which I could attach the feelings. They just floated there above my head like the dark cloud above Charlie Brown's *Pigpen*.

My walk home from the Fayetteville bus station felt good – packed with relief. It seemed to me that relief should

114

represent the opposite of 'packed' but my sense was not one of lightness or disengagement – just a solid, positive, palpable, entity that even represented some degree of joy for me. The sun had been long set and parts of my familiar route – the depot was along the path I took to Rick's Café – were pitch dark in the moonless evening. The uneasiness that presented did not detract from my generally positive mood.

Uneasiness was such a well-engrained part of my life I treated it like tight shoes – it was there, it was discomforting, but I could still go about the necessary tasks presented by my life.

Once home I turned my attention to Geneseo. I found the college website. The city – town – had one as well. In preparation, the night before I had drawn rough renderings of landmarks I thought might appear on those web presentations. There was the large, grassy, quad enclosed on three sides by buildings. There was the entrance to the 'Old Main' building. The campus sat on a hillside and I drew the extremely long set of steps that ran down from the quad to the dorm area below. I made a rendering of the main street indicating several things I remembered about it – a corner hotel, small and white – a barber shop, a grocery store, the firehouse. My life there would have been some forty years before so I expected landmarks might have changed.

I went to the city site first. What can I say? The main street was still narrow and lined with hundred-year-old buildings. Perhaps my rendering was enough of a match. I couldn't really say. I seemed to remember something about the summer festival which was pictured but that was one of those after the fact visions and I had determined I couldn't really count on them as 'evidence'.

The college site offered the support I required – the quad, the steps, old main, were all there as I had pictured them. As I scrutinized every pixel, a name came to me – Dean Park or Parks. Even a fuzzy image of his face came to mind. I found the history page and read it with interest. As an arm of the State University of New York, the college's chief officer had not initially been a President but a Dean and Dean Park had been the last one before the position had segued into,

115

President. The dates of his tenure coincided with the dates I figured I would have – could have – been there.

Another vision floated by. My young son and I were in the Dean's cherry orchard. I was steadying him (my son not the Dean) on the stepladder as he reached out and grasped a cherry. He was surprised when it came off in his hand and he tried to reattach it. It was a wonderful moment. Again, I looked so young. My boy could have been no more than eighteen months.

I had no way of verifying the cabin on Lake Conesus. As I thought about it, though, I saw a winter scene. The cabin was down a sharp rise from the blacktop that led to town. The memory extended. With snow, it was too slick to park the car down near the cabin so it was left up along side the road. Well before sun-up every morning the snowplow would come along and cover it in snow. Every morning the three of us would go up and dig it out. My memory was that neither my wife nor I seemed to be bothered by the routine. It was just how it was. The snowy season seemed endless there.

As an interesting, unexpected surprise that memory chained into one about George Peabody College for Teachers, a time honored school in Nashville, Tennessee. Again, my mind presented a few images, though not as clear as those from Geneseo. Again, there was the quad – the largest I could remember ever seeing. I remembered the Psychology Building. I saw barrack like buildings. It seemed we had lived in them. I supposed that indicated student status rather than teacher status. Perhaps that is where I went for my advanced degrees. I heard a tiny voice saying, "Peabody, house two." It held no immediate meaning but should have I thought.

Again I made some rough drawings before I visited the website. I was surprised to learn that it had become a part of Vanderbilt University. I looked through the history. If I had obtained a degree there, the merger would have occurred after I was there. My drawings were a good enough match to the photographs. I had no tags in time – no names of deans or presidents or professors or such. Nothing to find or investigate. The feelings I associated with the campus were

116

not particularly pleasant. In fact, the aura was of greatest disappointment. Overwhelming disappointment. There was nothing else. I might assume it had not been a good experience.

I was tired so went to bed. No wonder I was tired it was nearly midnight. My biological clock was set to nod off at nine.

I had another dream. It would fall on the not so good side of the ledger. I had lots of dreams but only a few, like the Bible guy with the needle, stood out as possibly noteworthy. In this one I was collecting (stealing, perhaps) heavy, probably decorative, glass objects – rosy/purple in color, the largest was no more than ten inches tall. The forms were meaningless but their value and importance were indisputable. I had them on a cart in a store that more resembled a large, open office area on an upper floor of some building. I draped them in a sheet or some such thing and moved with them onto the elevator. On the narrow, Chinatown-like street below, I moved clandestinely in and out of shallow buildings pushing my cart. I left it somewhere and returned to the 'office'. A woman immediately confronted me telling me she had proof from the surveillance cameras that I had stolen the valuable glass items. I was terror struck but yet immediately mounted a denial having to do with somebody – the assistant manager – forcing the cart onto me as I entered the elevator. There it trailed off into nothingness. I felt extremely threatened by the woman's accusation and relived the feelings as I relived the scenario. Having been caught surprised me completely. It was not my thing. It didn't fit my picture of myself or the picture others held of me.

I had no helpful associations with elements of the dream, only faint interpretive possibilities. Rose is the color of anger management and glass might suggest transparency or fragileness. Milky rose might represent the frustration of not being able to see clearly into them – them being things that were obviously meaningful to everybody at the moment. Perhaps the rose in the milkiness – which impeded my ability to see in or through it and which could cause great consternation – might work to ameliorate the angry

117

component. That's probably a fantastic reach. My apologies, Sigmund. The pieces were really not fragile. In the dream the purpose of the pieces was clear to everybody – even me (though I don't remember what that was). Although I was picking up the pieces in plain sight of everyone, nobody commented about it or seemed in any way bothered. I remembered feeling I was easily getting away with the robbery.

Later I would put on my psychologist hat and see if any truths seemed self-evident. I understood that it *had* been a dream. I had not lived it or if I had the version I received came in the form of a dream. That presented some degree of relief for me because I had a growing concern about how well I had been drawing an accurate line between reality and fantasy.

There had been another dream. The remnants of it came to me later in the morning – by then a faded image I was sure. It was an Elliott Ness type, G-Men vs. gangster, setting. I was in a very dark alley dimly lit by a single light bulb high on the side of a building across the way. The leader of the Feds exited his vehicle and shot me with a sweep of fire across my lower abdomen from a 'Tommy Gun'. The flashes from the prolonged burst of fire lit the alley – perhaps brighter than reasonable. I told him he had made a mistake, that I couldn't have been the person he was after. He said he was sorry, tipped his hat, got into his 1920's car and drove off. The memory stops there. The attached emotions were intense but fairly matter-of-fact – more sad than either frightened or angry. Some degree of elation worked its way into the odd patchwork of feelings. There was something of extreme importance connected with the machine gun – something about it that lit up my life there in the darkness. I wanted the brilliant bursts to continue even though the result would clearly be devastating. I couldn't pin it down. Its image haunted me for months – awake and asleep. It remians clear even today.

Finally, with my 'new' life believably founded in the Joplin experience, I felt more secure. I questioned less my ability to keep my reality and unreality files straight. I now envisioned three kinds of memories: those I could prove with solid data, those I could not prove but even so believed, and those that seemed likely to be false. There was a fourth category, of course – those un-memories that were still shrouded in the darkness of my mind. They had to be there, didn't they?

I approved of the concept, *darkness,* for it implied things were there but I just couldn't find them. It was more comforting than holding to the idea they were gone. In a dark room I could move about and bump into things. Manipulating them or feeling them I could determine what most of them were. I was counting on that same process to prevail in my life. I just needed to keep bumping into things deep inside the darkness of my mind until I found some key element that I could recognize.

The thrust of my search had been on discovering my name. I believed that held the key to unlocking things. Perhaps that had been the wrong strategy. Were there others – or at least one other – that might hold more promise? The names I had assigned to my wife and son were in the maybe category. Had they been accurate I believed more data would have surfaced to attach to them. That had not taken place.

I took out the two pictures that had been in my wallet that first day. They both still seemed familiar. Could they both be sons? Could they both be friends? Could they both have been patients? It was possible they were merely random pictures that I had added to my wallet to provide some legitimacy should I need it – if I were to be picked up by the authorities or some such thing. It was too nebulous to be meaningful.

Let's play 'what if'. What if one was a friend or patient and the other my son. Which felt more like which? I studied them for some time. The black and white photograph looked professionally posed and shot. That might indicate he was my son – somebody for whom I was willing to lay out that kind of money. The color picture looked more like a school picture. That seemed more likely to be from an acquaintance – friend, patient, neighbor, nephew maybe.

The feeling sense became greatly confused through that

119

characterization, however. The color shot felt like a very, very, close friend. Somebody I respected and counted on and loved to the depths of my being. The other also seemed like a friend but there were irritating, pricklies associated with it – with him. That second one presented a mixed bag – deep concern and caring, and yet the desire to build and maintain some distance. Those were feelings I hadn't drawn from the pictures before. Hair! There was something about each of them associated with hair. It was not a pleasant thing. I couldn't extend the feelings into memories or any sort of concrete data.

Still, there was a very positive side to that experience. I seemed to have been able to sort them though at a feeling level – at an emotional memory level. Maybe if I could level the visual playing field somehow – render them both in black and white.

I went to the computer and searched for ways to accomplish that. Scanning and saving the color shot as black and white didn't provide the similarity I needed. Eventually I found a program that transformed each of them into somewhat stylized, pointillism-like, pieces: the dots were replaced by short, horizontal, strokes. It put them into identical form. Although it provided no immediate revelation for me I really liked the pictures. I used the same process to 'fix up' a school picture I had of Wayne at about the same age and the three, contained in individual. 8 X 10 inch, oak frames soon hung behind glass on the front wall of my apartment. Three important faces in my life, only one of which I could imbue with actual memories. I put Wayne in the center, irrationally hoping his known presence might spread into the others. Like I said, it was fully irrational. When things were bad, I could view that wall and the icy cold prickles would warm and mellow. It works to this day.

My mind returned to the thoughts and feelings I experienced during the bus trip. It had been a fully engrossing reaction to the sounds, the smells, the gentle vibrating of the bus as I entered it and took my seat. The scene out the window there in the depot was familiar – dirty gray walls, a row of windows just below the ceiling, the bank of lockboxes, the dim illumination, the people – many unkempt and poorly dressed, reeking of cigarette smoke and alcohol. I didn't fit into that picture and yet there I was feeling a kinship to it all.

The overall setting felt familiar. Had I been a professional man prior to Joplin, bus travel would most probably not have been a part of my life. Maybe it stemmed from memories further back in time – as a child, perhaps. My memory was that of living as a poor kid from a poor family. It seemed reasonable we might have traveled by bus. It presented a possibility but nothing close to an explanation. Like so many of the pieces, *that* one would have to be put aside waiting for the suitable configuration to emerge so it could be at last cozied into a perfectly proper fit.

In my reconstruction, Ginny – who I eventually married – had been my very best friend from as far back as I could remember. As little kids we skinny-dipped together, climbed trees, hiked the wood, and mustered our courage to explore the Pickford Place – Manchester's version of the classic haunted house. As teenagers we bowed to the swim suit convention, volunteered to help the old folks in our community, talked with each other about important issues, and solved World problems – wondering how grown-ups could be so ignorant and hoping that 'adult ignoramacy' as we called it would not be visited upon us. At nineteen she proposed to me. Through my initial shock I blabbered to her that I didn't want to marry anybody I knew.

"Of course you do. Everybody in town – except you – has known we were meant for each other for years."

"Really. Hmm?"

Two months later we were wed. (Total cost: $7.50 – five for the license and two fifty for a bouquet! We were in love. What more could we have possibly needed?) Years before, as thirteen year olds, we had pledged to each other that we would remain celibate until we were married – not considering, of course, that it would be to each other. It was the teaching of our church and we both believed that arrangement held the best potential for a healthy social order and family structure. Whether it accomplished those things or not I am no longer certain, but one thing was for sure, it made for one absolutely, unbelievable, trip to the edge of the Universe, fantastically joyous, wedding night!

Surely *that* had to be a 'real' memory although I do recall I could whop up some wonderfully helpful, erotic, fantasies as a teenager. That was long ago and far away. I had no solid evidence and the only other person who could verify it was dead.

I was *really* tired of this not knowing most things for certain. I wanted to find somebody to gripe at about it. There was no one, of course. I needed to get back to living my new life. I needed to continue filling it with real things about which I could feel good. I needed to stop wallowing in the seemingly unknowable mysteries of my past. But, my, how I didn't want to believe this was all I was ever going to have. I didn't want to live the rest of my life without a past. I needed to know my story for sure – the real, honestly rendered, historically accurate, uncensored version. I needed that anchor firmly planted back in 1938 or whenever. Not having it had become the second greatest sadness of my life.

Alternatively, perhaps I should be happy about things as they were. If I had indeed done some horrific thing, uncovering it might devastate me. I would then have the dilemma of turning myself in or not – perhaps, depending on what had happened. I had considered that possibility many times before, however, back then I had no tangible reason to believe it might be true. My recent dreams – the Bible guy, the rose glass, Elliott Ness – all seemed to be presenting something new and different. None of those suggested any personally or socially redeeming characteristics within me. None even really shouted any objections on my part to my being caught or killed. Also, none suggested remorse for anything I might have done. The rosy-glass dream suggested my horror at being caught but that was more attached to the ruination of my good name I think as I look back on it. The ruination of my good name. Yes. What about that? Something. What? Nothing!

My basic pillars of my personality have been quite consistent during my Joplin-plus life. I have been a person of integrity. I am compassionate to a fault and give 'til it hurts. I am more tender than tough, more helpful than blaming, more loving than violent. In fact those second alternatives just never really surface even in mild forms. I tend to prefer the life of a loner but am not bothered by being with people or even by presenting programs for groups. Perhaps I choose to be alone because I have become comfortable with hiding myself and protecting others. I really dislike mindless chitchat as so often seems to occur at social gatherings, dinner parties, and such – who did what to whom with an unrelenting barrage of unsubstantiated opinions. The general ignorance displayed in such settings about the facts of the world, society, and the universe is both frightening and revolting to me. People who don't sincerely seek after knowledge and its continuous clarification scare me, and the world seems to be packed with them. More and more people are becoming more and more certain they are absolutely right and everybody else is wrong. (A typical reaction to extreme uncertainty about one's characterization of the Truth.)

If that makes me a snob then I suppose that's what I am, but I'm a snob who agonizes over the survival of my human species well past my generation; I agonize over poverty, illness, famine and illiteracy; I agonize over groups who are unwilling to strive for peace along side those who differ from themselves in background, belief, or origin. I can see no solutions when the world is dominated by unconcerned, uninvolved, my-way-is-the-only-way kind of people who are so quick to hate or isolate themselves from the essential problems of the day. Still, each day I do what I can to make my corner of the world better and more humane than it was the day before. *That* is, I suppose, what has kept me going these past eighteen or however many years it has been since I entered this otherwise thoroughly dominating darkness.

I would like to think that I believe all those problems are of such immense, ultimate, importance that my own are fully insignificant by comparison. I am not able to be that altruistic, that selfless, that fully other-focused. I don't really fault myself for it but do get royally ticked off when I see so many around me who just don't give a damn about anything but themselves. I can't understand, for example, how anybody

123

could, in good conscious, throw a sweet sixteen party for their son or daughter that costs thirty thousand, one hundred thousand or three hundred thousand dollars when there are undoubtedly people within a few miles of their home who are going hungry, are unable to pay for needed medical care, who are illiterate, and on down a long and sad list of social and personal maladies.   I just can't understand such a self-centered, uncaring, fully detached, way of thinking.   And, more sadly still, what will be the working philosophy that all those sixteen year olds will be carrying into their futures? Don't even get me started on the exorbitant amounts regularly diverted from truly important aspects of being human to be squandered on weddings and funerals!!!

I ramble – I rant and rave might more accurately characterize it.   Sometimes I wonder if my indignation is merely a diversion from my more personal concerns. (Sigh!) Maybe I used to be the guy who gave hundred thousand dollar parties. I can't believe it but I have no hard data. Maybe I'm reacting to my previous excesses – as if trying to make amends. Speculation.   It can't really be helpful – unless some of it triggers that keystone memory.

I have spent my last fifteen or more years creating fantasies in the books I've written. Now I wonder if some of those pieces of fiction might be true pieces of my life. It's been said a writer cannot divorce his writings from himself. I'm sure that's true. Am I the teenager trapped in the, huge, dark, cave with my archenemy?   Or, am I, perhaps, the archenemy? *(Disaster at Disappearing Creek)*. Am I the son of the single mother who struggles to come back from his terrible accident or the man who beat him to take revenge on his mother? *(Family Portrait)*   Am I Jay, the 10-year-old mortal boy or Twiggs the Little Person teen, or Gramps the wise old sage?   Probably all three, actually. And how about Detective Raymond Masters with his portly profile, kindly demeanor, and dogged determination to solve each mystery that comes his way. I have to assume there is a great deal of me in him – and more than a tad of wish-fulfillment going on. It is the series of *Ozark Ghost Stories* staring Marc Miller for which I can't see the connection. I'm not a supernatural kind

124

of guy. Perhaps that's the point – debunking the realm of the malevolent apparitions, except that never fully happens in those stories. Maybe I'm asking myself a very personal question. I really like the character. Maybe I'm merely reviving my youth through him.

My favorite characters are definitely the boys. I loved being a young boy. I loved the freedom and the minimal responsibility. I loved being the darling of my small community. I loved bopping along from one breakfast table to the next most mornings, chatting and carrying the best gossip from home to home. I loved confounding the adults with questions they saw as being beyond my years. I loved fixing things and relationships and people. Now, I love building those characteristics into the kids about whom I write. *Zephyr in Pinstripes* I have believed was, in fact, me at age nine. The youngsters in *Replacement Kid, Secrets of the Hidden Valley, Kidd's Grand Adventure, The Chipper of Oakton Villa,* and *Ripples,* plus the kids who 'assist' Detective Masters in his mysteries all reek of how I believe I was at those various ages. *Tommy Powers* the nonviolent, thirteen year old superhero is probably a lot like how I wished I could be at twelve or so.

Kids just show up in what I write. They wriggle themselves into places I hadn't intended. They come to the rescue of my characters. Sometimes they even become the co-star where none was intended (*The Mystery of the Barina Ruby* – a short novel within *Milieu: A method for writing novels and short stories).* I suppose if I had spent my former life working with kids and teens that may be a connection – an attempted bridge, even – to my past. Perhaps some of them show up as my characters. That would be nice.

Maybe if I were to re-read the books I would find that elusive door that would open and bring light into the dark that sits heavy within me. They didn't at the time I wrote them so why now? Am I grasping at straws or listening to new possibilities – new suggestions – from my Deep Mind?

The droning repetitiveness of my quandary and the disagreeable, soul scorching feelings associated with it must, I fear, make this a thoroughly uncomfortable if not boring piece to read. Page after page I seem to be saying the same thing: "Help me find a way out of my horrifying darkness. Provide that essential, elusive piece to the puzzle. Make my terror, uncertainty, and great sadness disappear in some legitimate way."

I understand that reaction because I have been living it every single day of my life. I, too, would like to close the book and walk away. The reader can. I can't. How fortunate and free the reader must feel recognizing that is his or her easily executed option. I have found no option that can liberate me from this unpleasantness, so must remain cloaked in my desperation, day upon day, night upon night, tear upon tear, into my eternity. (There I go again, see?)

I have to believe that my situation is fair in the grand scheme of the universe. I can't explain why my life has become what it has become but if I give in to the opposite belief (unfair) I fear my world will crumble. Life has to be meaningful and to be meaningful it has to be reasonable. With reason comes a sense of fairness. Some nights as I cry myself to sleep it seems so hard to hang onto these beliefs. It would be so easy to just let go and live – or die – with the unknown consequences. So many times I have walked to within a few yards of police station doors only to turn back as the anxiety of needing the answer is eventually exceeded by the terror of knowing. It is an odd dance in which those two are engaged. The yes-I-must-know partner twirling them toward the light of center stage while the no-I-dare-not-know partner changes course and hurries them back into the darkest corner.

More and more I am questioning the grand scenario I have painted for myself about life before Joplin. Bits and pieces have been shown to be true but so much remains unsubstantiated. I love the history I created for myself. Upon close scrutiny, however, it seems just too perfect – too complete, too ideal. I know of no one who has lived such a seemingly flawless life – well, seemingly flawless up until those last few, horrific, hours there on the red-stained lawn.

It has been the one thing I have had to cling to. Much of me – perhaps most of me – does not want to learn anything that might change that picture. What would happen to 'the

126

me' if all that were to crumble? Perhaps that is why my Deep Mind won't unlock the secret – it has heard my plea and is working hard to protect me from having to experience that change, that reversal in comfort. However, to cling to that history is to prevent me from establishing the truth – maybe?

It appears I have a huge, frightening, question to answer. If I choose to allow myself to become free from my ties to that comforting story, will I be strong enough to face the truth? How will I know if it is the truth and not just a second attempt at finding a believable base around which to center my life? I don't know. I just don't know.

My pillow will certainly lay damp this night.

CHAPTER SEVEN
The Way Back

Life went on. It seemed easier and easier to become resigned to the fact that the life I had was the only life I would ever know. It gave birth to long, dark, fingers of depression that reached out when I wasn't looking, which tried to gain a hold on me. I dispatched them though not always with ease. To work at finding my past seemed to open a window through which those fingers could gain access to my mind. I arrived at the place where I ceased all conscientious efforts to regain my past. My goal became building the very best life I could in the here and now. I tutored. I arranged more time with Wayne. I volunteered. I wrote everyday. I searched for ghosting and rewriting projects. I walked and even loafed.

I did my best at work (my job), although my efficiency there had fallen off dramatically over the past ten or so months. My 69 year old brain didn't handle multi-tasking very well anymore and most of what my station did, involved multi-tasking. Work on an invoice and be interrupted by the phone. Begin running a credit card and be interrupted by the phone. Begin anything and be interrupted by other folks needing information I had in my database. All of those things were reasonable. Each interruption brought new things for me to remember to do – and more opportunities to forget them. More people were added to the staff there and the small, cozy, comfortable work force that I had enjoyed (most days) outgrew my comfort level. They were all nice people but it made for just too many interrelationships. Too much background noise. Too much of too much. I tried to quit – thinking it would be welcomed, as many mistakes as I was making – but that was rejected. More accurately it was not accepted. They redefined my job description, dummying it down to something I could handle. It was a very uncomfortable event in my life – having to come to grips with my failing mental abilities. I could just see the tentacles of my depressive tendencies warming to my struggle. I fought back and with planning and effort reached a point where I was again proudly sporting a positive outlook on things. I made my supervisor promise he would tell me when my useful days were over. He agreed and I am confident that he will. I felt better. I was on his clock and I felt a huge load of responsibility lift.

I still really didn't like the work setting but felt I needed the money so would stick it out for a while longer. Becoming old and less competent was a part of life. I just needed to learn how to put it all into proper perspective and live with it. I'd think I would enjoy the lessened responsibility. With it came fewer failures and that should translate into fewer bad feelings about myself. Instead I felt as though I was being protected from my inabilities. Patronized. It wasn't positive.

At home my writing continued to go well. I realized that, more and more, I had begun depending on the thesaurus in MSword for the alternatives that used to just slip so easily off my mental tongue. I appreciated the help but regretted the dummying down of the task for all of us who wrote. What motivation did youngsters have to acquire a large vocabulary rich in alternatives – shades of meaning, texture, emotion – when they could just right click a word and be deluged by dozens of possibilities? I suppose, even so, one does have to know the subtle variations in the meanings of the words before making a fully appropriate choice. Since I first became fascinated with the wonders of language I have been awestruck by the subtle differences among supposed synonyms. The manuscripts that are submitted to me for re-

130

write suggest that knowing such subtle nuances is a rapidly declining skill.

I suppose those last few paragraphs were filled with material that seems only tangentially related to my story. Perhaps they reflect my rush to disengage myself from the all-consuming search I have been describing here. Perhaps it represents a kind of freedom I now experience relative to the kinds of concerns I can allow to consume me. I hope it is not making me less careful than I may still need to be. It seems I am determined to establish a normal life and let things fall where they will. I hope that is not an irresponsible approach. If my mind is going to give up its secrets it is clearly going to do that within its own time frame. It would not be truthful to say I have given up thinking about my past, the mysteries that are still hidden there, and my deep desire to remember every nook and cranny of it. I have, however, come to feel less desperate about it. I am me and I have come to really like the me I have learned I am. (So much for *my* part in stemming the fading art of conveying the subtleties of language!)

Perhaps it had to do with my easing up about it all. Perhaps it had to do with the way in which my probing and re-probing of my Deep Mind riled things up and drove them to the surface bit by bit, fleeting image by fleeting image, unique emotional reaction by unique emotional reaction.

Regardless . . .

That brings things up to '*The Grand Awakening*' as I have characterized it. As I think back to those first moments, it still engenders shivering cold sweat wrapped in the greatest joy I can imagine. Again I can pinpoint the day and hour.

That evening, like all those other evenings I have been recounting, I went to bed with no real, for certain, verifiable, name and only a few years of personal history. That evening, like all those others, I sobbed myself to sleep. That evening, like the others, I had no real expectation that when I awoke anything would have changed in any meaningful way. I would squint my world back into focus. I would yawn and stretch myself back to life. I would reach for a corner of the sheet to use in drying the side of my chapping face as I turned it up from my dampened pillow. I would scratch the

131

dependable morning itches and sigh the sigh of all sighs as the sadness of my gloom flooded back across my consciousness. I had grown to cherish that minuscule moment between sleep and wakefulness before I remembered. I would try to prolong it but of course such an attempt, itself, precluded such innocence.

Here is how I recorded the experience as it unfurled (edited for structure, later).

2:11 AM, November, 20, 2006

"I just now awakened. I suddenly understand the meaning of a cold sweat. I found myself sitting up in bed, speaking aloud. I believe I am remembering my real name – something that has eluded me since that morning on August twentieth, 1990 – when I suddenly found myself with a suitcase and a duffel bag heading south on the back streets of downtown Joplin. At that time, it was as if I were emerging from a fog of nonexistence. It was terrifying. It was fascinating. It was fully unreasonable. I have been learning to live with it, collaring it with brute mental might and evading it through my escape into the complexities of the characters and twisting plots in my novels. *But tonight!*

". . . I have now moved to the computer to try and record all of this as it tumbles out of my mind.

"The name that is screaming at me is Thomas David Atherton – Tommy, Tom, Tom-Tom, Tom the Atom Bomb. I know it is right. This is exciting beyond words. I'm spraying tears as I sit here trying to type. My heart is racing. I can't fully assess my emotions – happy, relieved, scared, giddy . . . All of those I suppose. I'm trembling. My typing is even worse than usual (Smile). Mrs. Boyd would again frown and shake her head in despair, uttering, "Tommy, Tommy, Tommy." Yes! I am remembering Mrs. Boyd, my typing teacher from High School! What a rush as the kids say.

"Scenes. Faces. Places. Bobby! Dear, dear, Bobby. It is all rushing in on me. I see family members and have names for them – real names I am certain. It is as if all of my time is happening in this single moment. I am a child coasting along on a red, wooden, self-built, orange crate scooter with roller

132

skate wheels. I am a man opening my office door. I am a high school boy shucking walnuts on a rise behind my rural home. I am surrounded by friends and happy laughter. Several familiar faces emerge within the group. Again, I am a boy – perhaps ten – with a new JC Higgins bike, bulging with pride and happiness showing it off up and down the streets of my small town, Carson, Illinois. I am a man sitting in a familiar studio in front of TV cameras doing a show – my show – *The Family Place*. Then I see me as a teen drinking coffee – two sugars and lots of cream – in a café at Rainbow Curve with friends – BL, DaVaughn, Dick, and playing a trombone in a wood paneled, rehearsal hall at school. I remember being on stage – a play, I forget my opening speech to the jury (Ayn Rand turned over in her grave!). I am in the driver's seat of a strange car in front of a Rochester, New York, hospital (Something Memorial – *Strong. Strong Memorial*). My wife sits beside me holding our new baby, Robert Franklin   It is such a big name for such a tiny little squealing, red, being. There is so much all at once. I won't be able to sleep anymore tonight. I'm going to go for a walk and just let things flow. I can't stop the tears. I guess I don't want to. I have known tears of despair for so long. I really don't want these tears of joy, elation, rebirth, to stop."

HOURS LATER:

"I must plan. I know I must proceed with caution since I don't yet know the why's and wherefores of my apparent amnesia (more accurately a fugue state, I suppose). I remember another dissociative problem as an adult. At one point I lost the capacity to speak. In therapy I discovered it was related to problems about wanting to leave my wife and, not wanting to hurt her, being unable to broach the subject with her, afraid of what terrible thing she might do to me or our son. And another time, back in college there were times when I would show up in places with no knowledge of how I got there.

"Oddly, I have no specific memory of actually leaving anywhere. It may have been triggered by some despicable thing – *to* me or *by* me – although knowing the person I have

133

learned I am, I have truly believed that I could not have been any sort of culprit. I must handle my reemergence with care and caution. So many questions. So few answers. (My writing is usually not that trite and stilted.) I'm not sure what moved me to add that disclaimer. Just now, I really don't care.

"During the past moment I had a very strange, anxiety filled, thought – realization – whatever. As I learn about my real past I will have to give up the one I constructed through hypnosis. It is obvious they are *very* different. My forced excursions into the deepest shadows of my psyche did not serve me well. I knew that was a possibility. I'm suddenly torn – not really wanting to give up what I have come to believe. It has been my rock – my comfort – throughout all of this terrible uncertainty. It could be characterized as *sick to my stomach fascinating!"*

*****

SEVERAL DAYS LATER:

Between then and now I believe the most important memories have returned – except the act of leaving and the motivation behind it. Things from my past seem to have fallen into place. I no longer believe that my wife and son were murdered. Where does that put them now? Alive somewhere I hope. The joy associated with that likelihood is boundless! I have a plan.

First, I will regain my identity – legally with social security card and state ID card. That has presented some difficulty since my wife apparently had me declared legally dead ten or so years ago (according to the SS office). So, I find myself in the position of having to prove who I am, a difficult undertaking since no one who knows me as Tom Atherton has had contact with me since I disappeared. I will have to take the bull by the horns and round up a few friends from my high school days in Bentonville to vouch for me. (Bentonville is a few miles up the road from here – the place I lived as a teenager.) It is scary but I am really looking forward to reuniting with them. My sudden appearance will be difficult to explain. I am sure I can come up with a plausible explanation. All this time I've been so close to

134

them, geographically, at least. I now understand why I have been so comfortable here. It is home.

The liklihood still looms, that the "mafia" story is true. If so, I could be putting myself or my family back in danger by 'coming to life.' I seem willing to risk *that* just to be able to reconnect with my real past. It seems so selfish as I reread it here. Perhaps it deserves a period of 'rethink'.

Things get even eerier! Fully inexplicable to me – and I mean mind-boggling, inexplicable to me – I found a flame-resistant lock-box on the floor of one of my closets. I don't remember it being there although it contains some tax forms and other material from my *new* life. Most inexplicable of all, inside it I found several documents relating to Tom Atherton. There is a copy of my birth certificate obtained within the past several years. There is a copy of my marriage license and a transcript from Manchester College both of recent acquisition. I have absolutely no knowledge of how I obtained them. The only answer would seem to be that part of my mind was moving in and out between the two me's and the JerryMe was not privy to the doings of the TommyMe. It was as if that part of my mind was preparing for my comeback – my breakthrough – my great awakening. It is as if good old Tommy was taking care of me all along. It seems fully implausible but at this time I have no other explanation. I'll keep searching, of course. The small, bronze, key to the box seems to have been on my key ring all along. I can't remember ever wondering about it.

Second, I must locate my family members and decide how and when to reenter their lives – Dad, if he is still alive, Bill, Larry, Bob, especially my son, Bob. I remember – vaguely – that my wife left me and went to live in one of the Carolinas. I still don't have that clearly in mind and hope what I remember about our generally unfortunate relationship is wrong. I don't remember a divorce. I suppose being declared dead is just as good – perhaps better. My feeling about her is a turbulent mixture – I truly loved her but I couldn't stand to be around her. Right or wrong I remember her as a suspicious and hurtful person toward both Bobby and me and I never understood why. I *really don't* want to meet

135

her again. I must assume that my absence may have worked some hardships on her, and sadness and distress on the rest of my family. For those things, I am so sorry although I feel no guilt.

Third, I must ease out of my present life and into my *new-old* one. Interestingly, stripped of the terrifying darkness, I love my life as it is, right here, right now. There will be huge decisions to make. I should soon begin receiving a social security check to help me financially in the years to come. There should also be some sort of pension from Illinois. As soon as I get the SS thing untangled I'll look into that. I may just end up being financially secure after all. That would certainly relieve one continuing, underlying source of tension. The picture of me flipping burgers for income at 93 – though humorous, as I see myself searching around for the spatula, which I'm already holding in my hand – has been frightening.

I will write more once my life has solidified or at least comes into clearer focus.

SEVERAL WEEKS LATER:

On a whim – not really I suppose – I contacted the authorities back in Wilton, Illinois, the town in which I had been living at the time I abandoned my old life. I felt the need to determine – solidify, verify – the date on which I 'disappeared' (for lack of a better term). A brand new, discomforting, mystery has emerged. I was told (I was using the guise of a writer researching the disappearance) that Tom Atherton was first reported missing in late February of *1988*. That was 32 months *before* I emerged on that back street in Joplin. Where had I been in the interim? What had I been doing? A disquieting uneasiness returns! Again, I wait. Again, I search. Again, I am dumbfounded.

Addendum to Awakening: (May 25, 2007)

Yesterday, I had a wonderful afternoon with Carole, long lost and recently found treasured friend from my high school years. She has patiently and dependably been helping me remember details of my life and has become my safe

136

haven and safety net. Every conversation brings new memories which burst onto the scene as we talk and then, later, settle into their proper places in my mind encouraging still others toward the surface. She refers to herself as nosey. I characterize her as compassionately, appropriately, helpfully, inquisitive. Each conversation brings relief as well as fairly intense anxiety. I have welcomed the anxiety because I know it surely must be a precursor to the dredging up of the final answers. Just to not have to be alone in all of this has been . . . well, I don't possess the positive superlative to describe how important it is to me.

As I lay in bed preparing for sleep last night I believe the final huge puzzle piece fell into place with a thud I am sure must have registered on seismographs within a four state radius. It is a terrible realization that provides both the greatest sense of relief and the deepest degree of sadness.

I have known there had to be some horrific event that forced me to block out my life and run away, hiding, fearing for my life all these years. Interestingly, a portion of it has been with me right along – part of the life I recreated through self-hypnosis. My mind washed it, bleached it, and hung it out to dry in a fashion, which I could accept, flapping there in the breeze more or less formless on the clothesline. Free from its dirt and grime and structure, however, it was useless in its reconstructive value to me.

I will recount some things already told. The sanitized version of the memory, which was 'left' for me was this: One of my teenage patients from the south Chicago region, turned out to be the son of a secondary crime figure. I became aware of that though not at the outset. During the course of therapy, the boy revealed to me many family secrets. He convincingly presented himself as hating to be a part of the 'family' and its activities. He arrived in a limo each week accompanied by his mother and bodyguards. He and his mother gave me permission to anonymously pass on information about the family's activities to the authorities, which I did. In my cleaned up fantasy, the authorities were able to investigate the very specific leads I furnished and bring down the Crime Family freeing the son and his mother. A neat, more or less happy, ending.

The kicker in my fantasy was that the father found out about what was going on. He sent his 'goons' to deliver his message to me. 'Leave now. Lose yourself in such a way that you disappear forever. They might or might not come after me. If I didn't leave immediately, they would begin hurting my young patients and killing my family members.'

It makes sense that I would leave given all that. It didn't, however, make sense that I would turn off all memories of that and of myself because of it. That has been my recent puzzle.

The *real* event, though similar, was a gore-dripping, horrific, nightmare that most certainly had the power to sever me from my past.

I *had* been seeing the son of a crime figure. The boy and his mother, however, were working in the service of his father. The information he had been feeding me was, in fact, about his father's *rival* crime family (a name the boy assumed for the ruse). Family Two learned about what Family One was up to (some inside source) and took swift vengeance. It was *their* 'goons' – not those of the boy's father – who visited me with the message to leave within hours and disappear completely – become invisible. The message was clear: If I were to surface within the next twenty years, my son and I would both be killed and my patients maimed.

Again, that was probably not enough to do the damage to my psyche that had, in fact, been visited upon it. It let me know quite clearly what I had to do (leave) and I would most certainly do it for the sake of those I loved. I was a strong person, mentally and emotionally. It had to have been something *even worse* than that. Again, I wondered if it had been the mere fact that I had to abandon my family and so many patients with no warning and no explanation. Maybe. Probably not. The 'goons' actual directive continued.

Even Worse # 1: A half dozen of my patent's families had been paid huge sums of money to file sexual misconduct complaints against me, thereby ruining my reputation and effectively closing my practice. I would not be around to defend myself. My flight would seem to be an admission of

138

guilt regarding those accusations. Few things, other than my loved ones, were more important to me than my good name and the honesty, compassion, and helpfulness, which that implied. It built an insurmountable dilemma.

Even Worse #2: During their brief visit, the bald 'goon' unrolled a full-sized, color, photograph of the 14 year old boy who had played the central role in the drama. He was lying in a casket, his severed head resting between his hands on his abdomen.

I had kept a diary of the boy's revelations and had not, in fact, passed them on to the authorities. I remember burning it before I left. I remember withdrawing all my money from the bank. I stuffed cash into several socks. I packed a minimal amount of clothing into a single suitcase. I left a note for my son, designed to cover my unexplained exit, and some signed checks for him to use, as payments were received from my patients. I got in my car and drove east. My intention was to reach the airport at Toledo, and take a plane to somewhere from there. I remember feeling a bit paranoid, not wanting to decide on the destination of that flight until I walked up to the ticket counter for fear 'they' were listening to my thoughts.

It is there my memory ends. The next thirty plus months remain a blank – until the morning I emerged on the sidewalk in Joplin after a bus trip south from Kansas City. Clearly I had been able to remain in deep hiding and survive those several years. Where or how I do not yet know. I can imagine moving often, working at minimal pay jobs or surviving out of the goodness of the kind souls who ran soup kitchens. I do not feel emotion attached to those months.

I am sure that other peripheral memories will surface to solidify this final piece of the puzzle. At the first realization of who I am (several months ago), the underlying anxiety that I had been carrying for so many years began to drain away. The difference between an overwhelming load and a light load sometimes fools one into thinking it is *all* gone. Yesterday there was a surge of gut wrenching anxiety that continued to grow right up until bedtime. This morning it has dissipated and I feel total relief for the first time in perhaps twenty years. I'm sure it cannot really be total with all of that time still unaccounted for, but as I said, from overwhelming to just a little, feels like Eden today.

One more, quick, note here this morning, after a night in which I alternated between sobbing and throwing up. I just spoke by phone with an archivist at a Chicago area newspaper. Even without the wonders of the computer age she was (probably) able to complete this part of the story for me. According to her recollection, both of the men who were most likely the warring 'fathers' in my life (given the dates, place, local street rumor, and so on), have since died mysterious deaths. Her take on it is that they had ordered each other killed. I feel free. I can understand the utter joy a slave must experience when his shackles are removed and he finds himself at liberty to move about the world as a full fledged human being. It is akin to the miracle of birth – rebirth in this case.

I find myself unable to sit. I excused myself from work at noon. (I answer the phone and do light clerical work there.) I pace. I smile. I cry. I ruffle my hair and twirl myself with wondrous abandon. I want to shout but it is not my style. I want to tell everybody but have thought better of it. Carole. I will certainly tell Carole. Then, of course, I must find my family.

I can't explain it but I have tremendous, chest aching, reservations about making that contact. I have most likely been dead to them. Should I leave it at that and not open old wounds? Perhaps I'm not dead to them – still just missing – in their minds regardless of the Court's edict on the dire state of my health (or un-health as it were). Most likely their feelings lay in that terrible no man's land of not knowing. I've lived through that for so long that I cannot in good conscience impose it upon anyone. How will they receive me? What about the rumors? There are always rumors.

First, I must locate them. The internet should provide that service in a swift manner.

LATER:

I was fully amazed at how many Robert Atherton's there seem to be in this land of ours. Unbelievable! I do believe,

140

however, that I have found one of my brothers and a nephew. My current plan is to contact the nephew first, hoping he can ease the news to his father and help me locate my son. I hyperventilate at the thought of making those phone calls. I can find no email addresses or, being the chicken I find myself to be, just now, I would use that as my first contact.

At this moment I can think of no greater joy than being again with my son. I must not mess that up. If I only knew for sure how he was going to react. I can't know that ahead of time, I suppose.

The feelings that eventually flowed from the picture of him (the one in color), which I have carried all these years, were those of love and respect and friendship. Even the darkness of my mind could not block out those things. I remember long talks between us after he became a man. I remember working with him to build my office/residence. I remember how we used to laugh. My, how I remember the laughter. I remember his wedding and his dear, sweet, wife. I remember being with them during the final hours I spent there in Wilton. The hardest thing I've ever had to do was say goodnight to him that evening just hours before I left. For him I assume it meant, 'See you in the morning'. For me it meant, 'Goodbye forever'. I managed to hold my smile as I died a bit inside.

I left him a note, as I recall, hoping to telegraph some element of my situation – poorly disguised, I suspect. I am a terrible liar. I have no recollection of its content. I see it there on a yellow sheet – maybe in an envelope with the signed checks. It is a blur and I suppose that is how I want to leave it. There is something else – nebulous and fragmented. Somebody may have actually dictated that note – or maybe several – and I copied it/them down. Blur. The scary guy. Blur. I'm at a loss for anything clearer. It was a long time ago and took place amid the most excruciating of all possible emotional upheaval. It seems reasonable that it might not have survived intact. There even could have been both – the one I wrote and the one I was forced to write. I don't know. Perhaps Bob will be able to help me with all that.

Before making 'the call' I went back to search the

internet one final time – procrastination, perhaps; anxiety, for sure. I tried a new e-mail search site. There it was: an email for my son. I had no way of knowing if it would be current. The several names associated with his in the description confirmed – I believed – that it was indeed my son. I copied down the address with great difficulty. I could not minimize the shaking of my hand. Eventually the eighteen or so letters and figures spanned the length of a sheet of paper. It was simple to remember but remembering accurately had not been my forte in recent years.

I composed a short message in Word so I could then cut and paste it into an email. I worked on several versions. In order to protect him, should the bad guys still be looking for me, I worded it in the third person and sent it from a strange-named account. I did my best to keep it from sounding ominous or scam-like in its presentation. I probably just succeeded in making it sound dumb. I don't know if I succeeded since at this moment it has been fourteen hours, thirty-seven minutes since it was sent and I have no response. My anxiety about it grows.

I just realized it is Fathers' Day, two thousand seven. It has been so long since I have really known myself to be a father with a real, flesh and blood, son. Just understanding that raises my spirits to a new high. My, how I hope he received my email and chooses to reply. I've been telling myself he may well be out of town for Fathers' Day – his wife's father or even his grandfather – my father, perhaps. Over the past several hours I have evolved a fantasy that he and my brothers and nephews have all gathered to be with my father – he'd be 102 so I suppose that's a reach. It would be wonderful, however. I want to be there – less for them, I am afraid – than for me. Again such a selfish stripe I am finding in my make up.

Earlier I was hit by an unnerving possibility. I have suddenly been filled with such an overflowing of love for my son. During the past few years, knowing as I did that he was dead, it has been the feeling I have had for Wayne. It is my hope that there will be enough for both of them. So far I feel no waning in either direction. I seem to have lots of love and

142

find it easily dispensed. I like that about myself. I understand that it was my way before the trauma and I understand that it has been the way I have been since. The terror could not quell it. The darkness could not hide it.

One of my great fears through all of this was that I might have been a very different sort of person before. To be that different would mean I would *not* have been loving, kind, helpful, giving, and compassionate. The vile trait pool that would leave for me was exceedingly disconcerting.

I feel no disconnect in my basic personality between before, during, or after. It has become a life affirming relief. I take some impish pleasure in believing that what I used to do for money, I have of late been doing for free. It is as though I have found a way to beat the major fallacy in the traditional care-giving system. I have come to believe that people with a talent – whether natural or acquired through training – have the duty to use it where it is needed with little if any requirement or expectation for payment. We are here to take good care of one another – first and foremost. I know, it will never float in our current money grubbing, me first, 'but I deserve it', society, but it is a wonderful dream. Only partially a dream, I guess, because it *is* happening here and there. I am not overlooking the fact we need to make a living.

I have mentioned the concept of *positive social values* often. It has become a thoroughgoing compulsion for me. It starts with the bottom line belief that the social purpose of mankind is to unselfishly take such good care of each other that our species will surely continue and flourish in safety, peace, mutual respect and blind-compassion for centuries to come. Most folks give at least nodding public agreement with that, feeling not to, makes them seem less human than they should be. It seems easily shelved in private. To accept that belief and not daily enact it in one's way of living is no better than not believing it in the first place. (My super-opinionated, probably rather snobbish, I'm-right-and-everybody-else-is-wrong sermon for the day – month – decade – life, I suppose. Shame on me?)

I have heard it almost everywhere. "I need to get ahead," or somewhat more desperately, "I just can't ever seem

143

to get ahead." When I hear it from someone who has few frills in his life, I feel great compassion and will do what I can to help. Usually, however, I hear it from the guy with boat payments, RV payments, payments on a house fit for three families, payments on the vacation, and on and on and on. What he is really saying is, "Because of all the frills I needlessly require in my life, I just can't ever get ahead."

Turning one's focus to helping the human race get ahead would throttle most of those complaints. Use what you *need* for yourself and use the rest for those who, for whatever reason, need it more than you. I tended to believe that back before Joplin, but I didn't really live it. I didn't really understand it at the level of kinship with all people everywhere. During these past eighteen years I've lived next door to those who were *really* in need. I brushed elbows with them at work. I've talked with them in the park and on the steps of their homes. At the depth of my misfortune – the day I had but twenty-five dollars to my name – I felt rich. Rich in the knowledge that I was fulfilling what I believed had to be the only logical, humanity-sustaining, social philosophy.

The lower animals really don't have a social purpose. Their's is strictly biological – live until old enough to reproduce and then protect your offspring until they in turn are old enough to reproduce their kind.

The human species, though clearly requiring that biological purpose as well, because of its great intelligence, its capacity for verbal thought and communication, its positively based emotions of love and compassion, and its several physical advantages over the other animals, has a required *social purpose* as well. Just as we can invent and create allowing us to survive the elements in relative ease, we also have the power to survive socially if we choose to. Some choose to live at the level of the other animals – kill or be killed, destroy those that are not like-minded or of your ilk, or selfishly preserve only your inner circle with no real regard for those on the outside.

I remember sitting in church as a small boy and hearing the minister tell the story of the snake species that died out because it ate other members of its kind and devoured its own

144

young. As I look at mankind today I see us as that species, mindlessly propelling us toward our own imminent extinction. The snakes may have been driven by uncontrollable instinct – nature's course somehow gone awry. Man has the unique and extraordinary capacity to rise above that if he will just look to the inevitable end of the path and employ his positive human potential. {See, *The Box*, for lots more.] (Okay, so the sermon wasn't over. It never is with me although I was fortunate enough to have a very wise father who pointed out to me that the behavior I modeled consistently each day was a thousand times more powerful than any sermon I could ever deliver. My 'sermons' usually employ fewer words and more action. Amen, or something, I guess!)

CHAPTER EIGHT
Waiting

Earlier it seemed so tempting to stay attached to the life history I created. It was so comfortable and trouble free. It had provided comfort and reassurance. My real life cannot be ignored, of course. After asking all the questions it became clear I had no choice in the matter. I must get my mental house in order. If I find I can't do it by myself then I will engage professional help. The first step seems to be to put down in black and white exactly what my true story is. Later, I will have my family members assess my memories about it – if I actually reconnect with them. Still no email. My disappointment grows.

As the wags say, I was born at an early age of mixed parentage – one male and one female. Actually it was to Lelo and Virginia, March 9, 1938, in Sterling, Illinois. My father was a school superintendent. I had two older brothers – Bill ten years my senior and Larry (Butchie as he was known early on) who is eight years older. I remember overhearing my mother tell her friend that I was, "An unplanned blessing." I figured that was good, being a blessing and all. Mother was the typical housewife of the era. She had ambitions to be a writer but for whatever reason never met with much success.

I spent the first three years of my life in Wickston, Illinois. Dad then took a position in Lorin. That is where my first real memories developed. I had two buddies in my neighborhood – Jerry and Bobby. There was also old Manuel and his two mules that pulled the ancient manure spreader that he used for his transportation. I can verify that the spreader smelled better than did the man – by a long sight. Adults saw him as a cantankerous old recluse. I found him to be kind and one who clearly enjoyed young people. Sometimes he'd let me sit beside him as we drove through town. We'd talk about all sorts of things. He had no teeth so I had to listen carefully. When we reached the top of the hill at the far edge of town, he'd stop the mules and I'd jump off, making a bee line back to my house across town. It was worth the long run to have had that time with the interesting old man. Mom would sniff me and ask simply, "Manuel?" I'd smile. We understood each other – she didn't fully approve but we understood each other. Most people never took time to get to know him. I suppose that was partly because he tended to be a recluse. Not really understanding about such things I didn't allow people to 'recluse' from me. I just waded in smiling and talking and asking questions – sort of innocently overpowered that loner tendency, I suppose. It is obvious that he became the model if not the essence for Arnie in my book, *Zephyr in Pinstripes*.

My oldest brother was very busy, as I recall. He worked at the grocery store on Saturdays and sometimes he would let me ride with him in the old black truck as he made deliveries. He made me feel important even through his impatience. Those hours are among my most precious memories. Mom may have insisted he take me. I don't know nor do I want to. The time was wonderful. Billy went to college the year I started second grade so our time together when I was small was pretty limited. Everybody said his was very smart. I'd watch him play on the basketball team. To me he was a great player. I remember that he seemed to spend a lot of time drawing naked ladies. I figured he was pretty good at it although truthfully I had no basis for comparison. They certainly looked lumpier than Brenda, Bobby's girl cousin who liked to play doctor with the three of us boys when she came to visit. I offered to pose blue jay naked for him but he turned me down. I suspected it had to do with my lack of lumps. I remember being disappointed.

My brother, Larry, was like my best friend. He taught me to ride a bike – a tireless effort that consumed most of a Saturday there on the gravel street to the south of our house. I remember how he boasted to my parents how well I had done – it had been said when he had no idea I could hear. That seemed to add a genuine turn to it and my chest all but exploded. I've often used that ploy since – bragging on a child when he thought I didn't realize he could hear. I remember that just after supper, most nights, Larry and I would wrestle on the dining room floor. I would be either Tojo Stumpbunk or the Great Biszzie Booszzie and he, Lampshade Miller. Those names, I assume, were the stuff of my ever-engaged, quirky, imagination. I'd always win and never questioned the authenticity of it. I remained closest to him until my college years when I lived for a time with Bill and his family while I attended Manchester College.

After Loren we moved to a farm north of Bentonville, Arkansas where I had a good friend named Tyke. I think it had been the plan for Dad to retire, but due to financial concerns we ended up back in Illinois come that September. I was never privy to the details. Dad became superintendent of schools in Carson . I was in fourth grade and cute as a bug. Life there was idyllic for a boy my age. Larry was a senior that first year and fell in love with a wonderful girl, Regina, who would become his lifelong partner. He went to the University of Illinois the next year and they were married. I remember how frightened I was for him when he joined the army. He played in the 5th Army Band and, not understanding it served ceremonial purposes safely within the States, I envisioned him and his band marching into battle with no guns to protect them. I cried myself to sleep more than once.

After seventh grade Dad 'again' retired and we moved to a farm south of Bentonville. That was not a good year for me. It was a much larger school than I was used to. Many of the boys in my class were two and three years older than I (the Arkansas schools seemed to retain kids multiple times back then). Some were even driving They easily manhandled me when I got in their way. (The damn, Yankee, kid). It seemed to be their delight. I suppose my being in with those older

149

kids was a source for the belief in my created life that I had been regularly, double, promoted. And why would that be? Because I was ridiculously smart. My memory is that of a terribly scary life that 8th grade year.

My freshman year was considerably better. Dad again came out of retirement to take the job of County Supervisor of Schools right there in Bentonville. It provided me with some instant credibility and eased my life immensely. I stopped being a nobody – a station in life I had never experienced prior to eighth grade – and raised me back to the level of a real kid. I made some good friends that year. I was in the band and orchestra – trombone – and came out of my shell. I believe I was genuinely liked by the other kids. I relaxed and enjoyed life. I was very interested in the girls but didn't know for sure what to do about it. Leslie, Larry, and Dick were my best friends as I recall.

Much to my amazement, on the first day of my sophomore year I was elected class president. Where had that come from? I stepped up and met the responsibility going on to be a leader throughout high school. My impression of me, looking back now, was that of an egotistical jerk. Those who knew me then don't seem to harbor that impression. I'm glad that my recollection of my intentions didn't dampen my positive relationships and apparent contributions.

Several of my junior and senior high school teachers made lasting impressions on me. Mrs. Rife, helped me understand I was smart, something I had really never connected with my high grades before. Grades had never been presented as an issue of importance in my home but they suddenly seemed to be everything in Bentonville. Mrs. Riddle pushed me to do my best. Getting A's was not the goal. I needed to move beyond that into a love of learning. I appreciate that to this day. Mrs. Barker – dear, dear, Mrs. Barker. She encouraged me to move beyond my own personal (often selfish) needs and serve the best interests of the larger group. It was one of the most important lessons I have ever learned. We loved each other. Duff Canady, was an unorthodox Presbyterian minister who demonstrated that I could live life my way and still make a grand contribution to

150

society. "Don't bend to other's expectations when they are fully unimportant in the larger scheme of things." Mr. Carter, my band teacher, taught me about responsibility and leadership and the importance of maintaining my integrity. Mr. Minnick directed the plays and was a Pentecostal minister. We were very good friends though our beliefs were quite different. In today's parlance he would have been considered cool. He could hardly bear that I was a Methodist instead of a 'true believer'. He once indicated that he was sure, however, that I would be the nicest soul in Hell. He taught me to look at things from more than just the *two sides* as is the usual admonishment (although that was clearly not really his belief).

During the second semester of my junior year I made a shift in friendships – not leaving my former friends behind but exploring associations with other kinds of kids. B.L. became by best friend. In many ways he and I were quite opposite – he smoked and drank, I didn't; he was sexually active, I wasn't; he swore, I didn't; he came from a poor, single mother home, I was middle class with two caring parents. We connected at the intellectual level. We pursued the big questions together – religion, war and peace, the proper role of government, sex (of course, we were seventeen), and on and on. We shared an interest in music. During our senior year I was class president and he was vice president (president of vice, perhaps!). We shared the leads in the class play, *The Night of January 16th* by Ayn Rand. Dick and DaVaughn rounded out my closest friends. Carolyn was my first true love. Dick was as bright a person as I have ever known and yet I have to wonder if he really understood that. Later, yes, but I doubt if it was a part of his self-concept back then. I always felt completely comfortable with him. After high school I had very little contact with anybody from my adolescent years but more than anybody else I remembered about my association with Dick.

At sixteen I obtained my lifesaving certificate and worked summers at local pools. E.L. became my closest summer friend. His family owned two resorts and it was at those pools that he and I worked together. We were very close and enjoyed each others company. He was extremely

151

bright. The fact that he came from a wealthy family was never any kind of consideration in my feelings about him. He was a fine person, we had good times together, we laughed a lot. Initially I really missed him.

My parents. Dad worked long hours with many evening meetings. He was always highly respected wherever we lived. From an early age I realized there was something very special about being his son and I took that quite seriously. I'm sure mother fostered that image. He and I didn't do a lot together – played catch, fished sometimes. I respected him greatly. During my second year in college I had some sort of emotional breakdown and came home to live for a semester. He and I became pretty close during that time. We went to the high school athletic events together (he had returned to Illinois to put in his last five years toward suddenly enhanced retirement benefits). I felt close to him during that time. Mom and I were always close. She was amazingly creative and I believe lots of that rubbed off on me via both genes and experiences. She encouraged me to try new things. People loved her and my friends liked being in my home when she was there. She could whip up a party in ten minutes flat. She died way too early. Dad soon remarried. He needed a companion and we boys were very happy for him.

Somewhere, in all of that family mix I developed the need to do well, to be successful, and certainly not to ever be at fault – traits that drove me but didn't make for the best adjustment, I suppose. I imagine it was largely do to pressures I began putting on myself – beginning in about 8th grade when I was feeling pretty down about me in most ways. I remember making a list that year of what things I would give to whom if I decided to commit suicide. It was all at arms length and quite 'pretend' yet I remember putting a huge amount of thought and effort into it. I assume my created life fantasy about my suicide attempt at sixteen probably grew out of that – that and my personal desperation of that later period in my life. As I recall I never came close to making any actual preparations to take my life. It does reflect my desperate loneliness and low self-esteem that year. I am reminded that Dad and I were really very close that summer after 7th grade. We were on a farm and milked cows together twice a day and played board games in the evening. We worked side-by-side remodeling some buildings there on our land and we put a new roof on the house. *That* part of my life that year was quite wonderful.

That first summer on the farm I had a friend a mile down the road. There was a creek on his place. We skinny dipped, and built a dam to make the swimming hole deeper and longer. That was also a wonderful part of my first months in Arkansas. Then, school entered my life and things plummeted.

After high school I spent three semesters at Manchester College. It was not a great experience. I felt trapped in some way. The ultra conservative religious philosophy preached by the college and espoused by the other students bothered me. It seemed so illogical that it put all religious thought into doubt for me. I didn't fully give up on it for a number of years but the topic caused intense unease within me and weighed heavily in my emotional breakdown.

I experienced a fascinating and yet terrible bind there. I had never known such wonderful human beings in such numbers before. They lived a loving, compassionate, positive social philosophy from morning to night. They, however, did so mostly, it seemed to me, because it was what their religion demanded (so they wouldn't go to Hell). For many it seemed to have very little to do with building a humanity friendly society. Assuring your soul's entrance into Heaven was always far more important than improving the lot of living people. It was impossible to talk about that with most of the students. There were a few faculty members who were willing if not eager to engage the topics with me privately (dear, patient, Mr. Merritt). The blind obedience to their faith bothered me no end. These wonderful, very bright young people were incapable of thinking beyond the religious beliefs that had been force-fed to them all their lives. None of it had come about because of their personal, intentional, studied, decision. The irrationality of it, the total disconnect between logic and religion, the lack of their ability to approach things in an open-minded manner, and their complete selfishness about getting themselves into heaven at all costs, caused my religion to implode. I left that college during the first semester of my sophomore year and, as I mentioned, recuperated at my parents' home in Flanders, Illinois.

As a note of interest to me, it was not the school paper on which I worked but the radio station. As a sophomore, I was the general manager of the station and did enjoy that. I had one very close friend – Don. It was then and with him that my interest in hypnosis burgeoned. I had dabbled back in eighth grade – one of the Little Blue Books. (It was from other books in that 'underground' series that my sexual education had, for better or worse, been established that same year. They were available mail order from some place in Texas. Ten cents apiece, as I recall. Name a topic and there was a book from which you could become fully versed.)

But I became sidetracked in that paragraph. Don and I read widely on hypnosis and used each other as practice subjects. We actually became quite proficient – three girls in my speech class threw up as I painlessly poked a huge needle through my arm during a demonstration speech. I haven't heard from Don since I left school. He was a very good friend during that very short period.

I spent the second semester with my parents in Flanders, Illinois and saw a psychiatrist a half dozen times or so – depression he said. Pills. I figured it was more confusion than depression. I can't be sure if he helped me or if the mere passage of time provided the cure. I worked the public pool there that summer and then entered the state college in Normal, Illinois as a sophomore. My unlikely major was geography – a secondary teaching degree was my goal – with double minors in psychology and social studies.

My friends there were friends for college and I had no illusions they would last beyond that. I'd been in such situations before. I solidified my philosophy of life during long, long, talks with Jay, an older fellow student, former minister (by then an atheist) and a fellow seeker after the truth. The questions we posed for each other fostered our growth. Recently I have been thinking about him often. I finished my BS in Ed there and began an MS in School/Clinical Psychology. I was married to an eighth grade sweetheart – not

154

a wise move on either of our parts and we each realized it early on in our marriage. People didn't get divorced back then – well, not 'good' people – so we gradually worked out a relationship. Like many a twenty year old male I had mistaken sex for love and her 'respectable family background' for emotional stability.

We got pregnant by design and we both loved the child from the moment we knew it was on its way. We later found that it provided several advantages for us in terms of my deferments from military service. Between that and pursuing graduate degrees, (we spent that first year in a masters program in clinical psychology at Bradley University), I fell through the cracks at Selective Service and had no military career. At eighteen I had registered as a conscientious objector and was given a 1AO classification – non-combatant. I gave that up for some special status designations as a student and then as a prospective father and later, father. It was mostly my wife who pursued those deferments and classifications. I would have been willing to 'do my time'.

The following summer I finished the masters that I had previously been working on at Normal, so began my first job teaching at Geneseo with two masters degrees – MA and MS. Two years later we arrived at George Peabody College in Nashville to begin work on my doctorate in clinical psychology. From there it was, interestingly, back to Flanders, Illinois, to serve as the County School Psychologist for five or so years. As I recall, I was pretty much the obnoxious know-it-all, being the only one in the county who really knew anything about the 'new' federal special education mandates. I did work hard there throughout the county establishing the special education program, leading the way to establishing a county mental health clinic, and serving on dozens of social oriented committees. I think I left a very positive mark on that area despite some viscous rumors my sick wife spread about me. She was given to doing things that got her the, "Poor Pat the martyr", response from others.

My wife and I also cared for numerous foster boys while we were there. Looking back I can see it was an unreasonable responsibility to thrust on her but she was an uncomplaining trooper about it. She became a somebody because of it and she always needed to be a somebody. Typically I'd bring home a teen-age boy from juvenile court and she'd take care of him. Well, that may be an exaggeration but the scales certainly tilted in that direction. They loved her and she handled them well. The second picture (black and white) in my wallet had been one of those boys. Why it was he that I chose to take with me I cannot be certain. I'm not sure that our 'help' really followed him very far into life.

From Flanders we moved to Wilton, Illinois and settled in for the long haul. I established a private practice of clinical psychology and worked in the elementary schools. I served as president of the International Association for the Study of Perception and made frequent speeches and presentations around the country. I contributed regularly to professional journals and devised numerous academic and learning disability tests, and training programs, some in association with my wife. We formed a publishing company, *Facilitation House* (now apparently incorporated as a part of *Slosson Educational Publications*). Things happened while I was 'away'. My hope is that it has been of some financial assistance to my wife.

As I have been writing the past several autobiographical paragraphs, I've been hit by a number of parallels between my real life, my created life, and the 'fictional' characters in my books. *Threads* might be a more apt descriptor than parallels. I was particularly delighted to realize that the characters David Lawrence and his nephew, Kit are most certainly based in my son and me. (*The David Lawrence Trilogy* – my middle name and my brother's first). In our last years together (my son and I) we engaged in wonderful give and take as do the characters. We talked about important issues and embarked upon a grand adventure (building my expansive office and home). We saw the humor in everything. We never considered that any obstacle might get the better of us. We joked and laughed and figured. We enjoyed being together. I was so proud of him as he doggedly pursued his education and showed himself to be a wonderful human being. The solvable-in-the-end adventures recounted in *The Box, The Map,* and *The Strap* certainly drew

156

me away from the terrors of my own seemingly unsolvable 'adventure' and allowed me to explore my fears and hopes in a safer venue. It allowed me to put my beliefs nose to nose with those, which challenged and opposed them, and see what resolution of the big life questions seemed most likely or reasonable. Crafting those thousand pages became my best therapy during the year in which they were written. They provided a sense of personal and philosophical strength – two elements of my life that I had certainly been questioning for many years.

I see myself in many of my stories. Through the old man in *Ripples* I was able to fairly succinctly and simply lay out my personal philosophy and demonstrate how modeling is more effective than edicts, requirements, and sermons. The boy is 'every-boy' – a composite foster son – I suppose. The story tries to anticipate the major questions with which youngsters must grapple, and talk around and through them while allowing differing conclusions to be legitimate after all was said and done. Think for yourself and be mutually supportive based in love, were the underlying tenets I suppose. Honest communication was certainly an important element. Don't push and shove your beliefs and values onto others is also in the mix.

I suppose those are the major elements in most of what I write. I mentioned it in passing before, how I believe each of the three main characters in *The Little People of the Ozark Mountains*® books are, in fact, me at different ages and different stages of philosophic development. Jay is me as the raw, naive though thoughtful, energetic, little boy. Twiggs is the construct of my idealism – some as a youngster but mostly as a teenager. His magical qualities are, well, just everybody's hope laden fantasy for personal power, me included. In the character of Gramps I was able to be more forceful in my 'sermonizing' because it was safely cloaked in the beliefs of an 'alien' culture and ordained by God, him(or her)self. Not often can I command that kind of authority!!! People love those characters and in so doing I suppose I conclude they love me. I've needed love these past two decades. I've seldom felt it, I suppose – well, there has been Wayne the past few years and it has certainly been a two-way feeling.

I mentioned Bobby, one of my early friends back in Loren. We fought daily but I admired him for one characteristic. He was absolutely fearless. When we were playing outside in the darkness of summer nights, he would bravely walk out into the blackest corner of the yard to fight off the dragon. It was the grandest show of courage I could imagine. I believe some of the Marc Miller character grew out of that. He is a writer who investigates ghostly happenings in the Ozark Mountains. He thinks like I think but is half my age. He approaches the most frightening situations with the courage of Bobby. So, we two early-graders, are still together in *Marc Miller, ghostwriter*. In *Ripples*, the old man described himself as 99% atheist and 1% agnostic. Marc is 99% a non-believer in the ghostly world but allows himself that 1% of possibility. In my philosophy I never absolutely disallow any possibility because more than proving myself right I want to be open to new knowledge and possibilities that may allow me to grow.

The young characters in my stories often begin as lost little lambs – a reflection, I have to assume, of the foster boys for whom we cared, and probably partially myself as an 8th grader. I have never felt a greater inner satisfaction than knowing I made a positive difference in a youngster's life. Several of my books seem to be based in that. All relationships, however, are two-way streets. Partners in a relationship always affect each other. I always grew from the kids in my life and in my books the same thing takes place. It is obvious in *Replacement Kid,* as the old janitor and the abandoned boy forge a bond and find ways to help fill the emptiness in each other's lives. In, *The Chipper of Oakton Villa*, the youngster takes on an entire retirement home and in so doing brings its residents back to life and helps himself come to grips with his own unspeakable secret. My kids are always upbeat. That may reflect my own temperament as a youngster – smiley faced, energetic, and helpful to a fault – or it may be a reaction against that terribly scary and depressing 8th grade year I had to endure. I want to use that year as the basis for a story but shy away from it, not wanting, I am sure, to have to explore the terror in anybody else's life – particularly a child's. I'm feeling strong enough to tackle that now. We'll see.

The junior high age boy in, *Kidd's Grand Adventure*, travels the country with his recently retired adoptive father. I believe it explores the relationship between my father and me that summer prior to eighth grade. It may also be a bit of a wish fulfillment piece – filling a void I felt for an adult male during the years leading up to high school when Dad was so busy. On the other hand it may have reflected my own deep sadness about not having a youngster in my life at that time so I invented one – one who was, as it turns out, a whole lot like the son I couldn't remember. Even in that book, however, I couldn't escape my own lot. An evil villain is tracking them as they move from place to place in the bus they have fixed up as their on-the-road home. The young readers seem to like that element of constant, lurking, danger so I can forgive myself for letting it sneak in. I must say my villains are real stinkers!

Last night as I reread portions of *Disaster at Disappearing Creek*, I suddenly saw so clearly the genesis of the two characters. One a wrong side of the track, less than athletic, early high school boy, new to the community, and attracted to the star football player's girlfriend. The other, that spoiled, star football player from a wealthy, established old family, with questionable morals and an ego so large it took an extra large helmet to contain it. He hates the new little squirt in town. As fate would have it, immediately after a terrible, blood drawing, rib cracking fight, they get trapped together inside a deep, narrow, slick sided cave. There seems to be no escape. They have to forge a working relationship if they have any chance of surviving. They work and talk and grow together. I'm rather sure I'm the new guy, much like I characterized myself in 8th grade – fully helpless at the feet of more powerful forces. The other boy is a combination of a bully who mistreated me that year (my lips are sealed) and my later to be dear friend, B.L. whose moral take on the world was miles from my own. Last night phrases leapt from the pages that I recognized were some that we actually tossed

159

back and forth at each other. The real life bully was more the ignoramus than the athletic character, and B. L. was more the intelligent, thoughtful part of the character as he emerged in the story.

It is just positively fascinating to me how those images and characterizations, sitting there walled up in my mind, would 'allow themselves' to be used and yet remain so completely hidden from me in all other ways. In one of the Raymond Masters books, *Gypsy Curse*, I actually named the high school age character, B.L. (*He* wouldn't reveal what the initials stood for, either!)

Crossroads, which is one of my favorites, has an intriguing origin. Back when I was living my created life and still, daily, trying to deal with the very real terror and sadness I felt over the loss of my wife and son, I decided it would perhaps be therapeutic to base a book with that loss as the back story. I wanted to move it into the future with a more positive outcome. The tale I told, remember, was that my family had been killed in a car accident by an intoxicated young teen and that he later killed himself. That second part grew out of a true incident from my real life. A fourteen year old in a community close to mine did just that. An elderly couple was in the other vehicle. A boy, perhaps my son, came to me soon after it happened and expressed concern about the boy – a friend of a friend sort of relationship. He was hearing things, which indicated to him suicidal recklessness and deep depression.

I contacted the boy's father and offered my assistance – gratis. He told me he had given the boy the beating of his life and it had been handled. He threatened my life if I ever approached either of them again. Six months later the boy put a bullet through his own head.

With that as background – hopefully not overly confusing as it wove back and forth between my several realities – the following plot developed.

The man who had lost his family (me, in my created reality) went in search of the boy who had caused the accident (his identity was not known in the story). My purpose was to provide some positive outcome for that boy. The man's initial

160

vengeful anger sets the stage for what I believe became an interesting and useful mystery/romance/drama. I began with only two elements – the man and his back-story, and the setting, a small, rundown café at the rural intersection of two little traveled blacktops. *'Crossroads'* comes to have multiple meanings. I knew the ending and envisioned it being a twist to be delivered in the final sentence of the book. It came very close to that. Then, as I needed characters to create the story and move it toward the conclusion, I planted them within the setting and watched them take on life and grow. It is my preferred approach to writing – story creation. (*Milieu: An exciting approach to writing*, 2007.)

Interestingly, though mostly based in the unreality I had created, the over-all, long term, effect on me was profoundly positive. The mind – what a fascinating thing. Later I used a similar technique – therapeutic activities with others – in which I would devise a dilemma with the person as the star and then had them work it out as a story. It consistently provided positive results.

Then there is the book that intrigues me the most, *Sanity in Search of Peter Alexander*. To tell any more would ruin the story and its effect, but the title coupled with what the reader already knows about me suggests the nature of the undertaking.

A few months ago, in the initial comparison I made between my created and my real life as a youngster, I was puzzled by the racial flip that was made in the personas of my 'parents'. After these many weeks of consideration I am inclined to conclude that I gave them – the most important and powerful people in a child's life – some aspects of the last person in my pre-Joplin life who wielded total power over me – the huge, terrifying, black goon (body guard). As my mind searched for a source of power, that character was certainly readily available. I cleansed him of his evilness, replaced it with love, kindness, and unselfishness, and he became my slightly plumb, ever smiling, black, 'father'.

In some ways the created belief that I married my best childhood friend was true. She and I were only really together during that horrendous 8th grade experience. We both moved to Bentonville that year and she and her family moved away the following summer. She and her family – friends from church – would come out to our farm most weekends to chop wood for their fireplace. She, her younger sister, and I, would roam our forty acres and just enjoy each other's company. It was total release from the terror I felt at and about school. There was never anything remotely romantic between us. I think the other kids thought we were a couple and I did nothing to dissuade them. Our families kept in contact and eventually – college years – my hormones urged me to write to her and see what might be there. Even all those years later the thought of her instilled a feeling of calm and safety and wonderful friendship. It blossomed and the rest of the story has been related – well, mostly.

I have still not received a response to my email. I sent a second one and wrote it from me, his father, searching for him. I used a different email address – a newly created one with my real name as part of it. Still nothing. It could be that it is not my son's address although I specifically requested that if the recipient was not he, I'd appreciate being notified of that. It could be that wrong person chose not to assist me by responding. It could be that my son is on vacation and not reading his email. It could be that he did read it and chose not to respond. Why not? Those possible rumors, perhaps. Maybe it all smells like some kind of scam. Maybe he doesn't want to reconnect. It is his decision, of course. I will not force myself back into his life. I just wish I could know one way or another. The worst possibility, of course, would be that he has died. I'm not going to consider that at this time.

I think I will write him a letter. I have found several addresses, which I am sure have been his at various times in the recent past. I may just go back to Plan 'A' and contact my nephew and brother. I will wait until the weekend before taking any further steps in case he is just momentarily out of pocket. Do I sound confounded by the situation? Goodness, yes!

There are still odds and ends for which I can't account. That Dairy Queen shirt continues to bug me. Now, I wish I had saved it. Somewhere along the line – when I was thinking of it as rag – I lost track of it. Then, there is that image of me leaving that house, walking the sidewalk down a gentle hill and catching the bus. I've tried to reconstruct what might have been written on the side of the bus, thinking that would provide some clue. I get nothing. I do see glimpses of what could be a small college campus across the street.

My belief is that those things are not random but in some way refer back to those 32 months for which I can't account. There is also that image of the airport, which I assumed was in Joplin. It may not have been, of course, and could be an element in those lost months. Would I have used my precious money on an airplane flight? If I took a plane out of Toledo during the initial leg of my 'adventure' (although *that* had been my plan, I have no memory of doing it) that image might be of the Toledo airport or the one at which I later landed. Where? I want to squeeze my head and force it all to surface.

I have also wondered if the dream about the glass objects might reflect a gift shop or some such place in which I may have worked. In the dream the setting was really more office-like. Did I work in an office? In the Bible guy dream I was clearly setting things right in a big, living room like setting – perhaps I worked as a butler sort of person in an old Victorian home. It feels like nothing but speculation. Using hypnosis I can force dreams to occur. My experience has been they are sometimes helpful, more as providing leads to explore further than for finding answers. It is worth a shot I suppose.

My hope has been that Bob might be able to shed some light on where he believed I went when I left Wilton. If he had known, I imagine he would have come looking for me. If the authorities launched any kind of search they either did a very poor job or, as a hider, I was exceptional.

That triggered a series of *new*, possibly related, thoughts. I breathe heavily as I capture them here. The first is me returning on foot to a medium sized, two story, yellow, motel and seeing a police car parked out front. I felt terrified and hid myself for some time behind a van. I waited until the trooper left before entering through a rear door. I called the front desk from my room to see if there was a message for me. There wasn't. I felt relieved.

163

I took a bottle out of a sack I was carrying. It was hair dye – auburn. I remember undressing and entering the shower to dye my hair. It made me look years younger – well, more my age I suppose. My gray hair had come upon me at a ridiculously early age. I felt younger. I remember how terrified I felt and how suspicious I was about everything – maids, taxi drivers, store clerks, even the youngsters who manned the fast food places (what evil intentions were those so easily flashed Cheshire grins hiding?). When in the shower I'd leave the curtain open and the door to the bathroom open so I could keep a look out.

Those are all just flashes of unfinished images. None of those memories fit into anything I have previously remembered – nothing Joplin or after. There is no closure. The scenarios go nowhere. The one all too familiar part of it is the terror. Wait! I see myself lying on my back on the bed in that motel room. I was crying, chest heaving, sobs. Terror and helplessness. As much helplessness as anything. It is an absolutely horrifying, end of the Earth, nowhere to go, all is lost sort of memory. It is so intense to this very moment that I must get up and go pace or something. Scream. Find mommy. As a child move to the safety offered behind my father's leg and hold on for dear life. I needed safety and quite clearly nothing I knew of or had ever known of could supply a sufficient amount.

My. That was fully unexpected. It is clear that considerably more really bad stuff remains inside than I had ever dreamed. Maybe it is best just left alone for a while – forever??? It has to be connected with those lost months. From my brief preview just now it would seem that period was unspeakably terrifying. It makes sense, if it was related to those first months when running and hiding and surviving and not knowing were all so new and confusing. I must have been so terribly lonely and so worried about my son and the welfare of my patients. The 'not knowing' aspect of that period must have been simply excruciating. If, in fact, I remembered nothing about the whys and wherefores, the emptiness must have been dreadful.

Ah! Not knowing – like right now, not knowing about

164

my son, his welfare and his reaction to my overture. That uncertainty could well have sparked the images from a time filled with similar emotions and distress. It is both fascinating and unbelievably uncomfortable. I think I need to let that just percolate on the back burner while I get on with my life.

My life. That presents an interesting conundrum. Today I have a life that is in most ways satisfactory. I have Wayne and Carole for however long. I really don't have that previous life anymore. I have decided that I don't want to go back to doing therapy for a living. Not having been licensed for so long would provide immediate and probably insurmountable problems, anyway. I want to write but I need to be able to sell what I write. I suppose *that* – marketing – needs to become my number one priority. Clearly I need a bippity, boppity, booing, fairy godmother to come and magically handle that for me. *Or*, just sit myself down, set a marketing plan, and hit the bricks myself. UGH!

I want to continue working with young people – probably something quiet like tutoring since my last outing skateboarding with them, came within a bruised behind of ending my life! I could teach swimming. I always enjoyed that. I have had a dream of opening a combination book and gift/craft store offering just Ozark authors and Ozark crafted gifts. I've seen such things come and go – bankrupt within a year. Not a great idea, I'm sure. The publishing industry is changing so rapidly. Maybe publishing E-books is the way to go. I can't imagine retiring.

I suddenly feel adrift. Previously, I had an overriding purpose, goal: stay hidden and survive. That was a pretty compelling set of tasks. My attention never (well, seldom) faltered. My focus had to remain clear. I had to remain alert and almost every day my creativity was challenged and had to be at the ready. It took nothing less than the contemplation of the biggest questions the human mind can ponder to keep me distracted from my relentless dread and the unknown terrors of my darkness.

But now, even though those unaccounted months still exist, I have choices and options that I didn't have before. My very life no longer depends on my ability to maintain the various tales I've had to concoct to explain myself, my past, my frame of mind. I am not ready to just toss out my current life so the need for those stories remains in order to maintain my ongoing social and workplace relationships. But it is no longer a matter of life and limb. With 'Big Tony's' twenty-year 'keep yourself hidden' time frame nearing its end, my fears for my family have pretty well evaporated. My belief is that the crime family now has concerns that are far more important than I am and that in fact my role in its life (all quite inconsequential, as it turned out) may well have been forgotten. Recent histories that I have been reading about the South Chicago area 'families' certainly bear that out. If this treatise is ever published and if I get whacked soon thereafter, I suppose my assumption was ill taken. (That doesn't seem as humorous written out as it was during its mental formulation.)

OH! My! What if the reason my son has not responded is that Big Tony did, in fact, have him killed. How could I possibly ever live with that? There it is again, that fully selfish streak! An overwhelming, terrifying, discomfort has overtaken me.

CHAPTER NINE
Loose ends

During the course of this account my various realities have mixed unreliably and faded in and out from one another. It will be my objective here to sort and organize some of those more elusive elements and offer some tentative (possible) interpretations. It has been pointed out to me that this may a singularly unique event – a prolonged fugue state by one trained in clinical psychology. I imagine it was. Sometimes that aided me, if not in promoting my immediate recovery, at least in understanding and patience as I lingered through seemingly endless months and years of disequilibrium. I had some resources to utilize that most other people would not have. They gave me hope and allowed me to justify not presenting myself to the authorities. Looking back, that might have actually been the best way to go. I could not have known that, however.

Those initial questions: One of my first quandaries concerned the series of questions I asked of myself at the moment of my conscious emergence in Joplin – age, president, date and so on. I didn't question their reasonableness. They are routine questions asked by psychologists and psychiatrists of disoriented patients to assess their degree of contact with reality. There was no doubt in my mind but that those were the appropriate questions to ask at that moment. It was part of my professional knowledge that had arrived with me fairly full

167

blown, if still cloaked in darkness. I wouldn't realize that until later, of course.

The Black Apple: The immediate emergence of the 'black apple' was a throwback to my earliest exploration of hypnosis. I remember learning that it was useful to establish a visual key that could trigger an immediate hypnotic state – especially when using self-hypnosis. I even remember the example in the book – 'green rose'. It needed to be something out of the commonplace so you wouldn't inappropriately begin to slip into a hypnotic state. 'Yellow Pencil', for example would not be unique enough. 'Green Grass' would not work. I chose black apple because it fit all the parameters necessary for such a trigger. It became a well-practiced point of focus that I had undoubtedly used thousands of times before. When I needed to relax, it presented itself immediately.

As a somewhat amusing aside relating to inappropriate triggers, I was once working with a super anxious boy – thirteen. The problem grew worse during school hours. I taught him how to develop a relaxation trigger in the form of the face on his watch. (In that case it needed to be quite obvious, everywhere present to be helpful.) Every time he looked at it he would automatically relax. Boys that age look for the time a hundred times a day. It worked like a charm in the classroom and at home. It had one unexpected down side, however. Soon after the technique was firmly engrained he was on the basketball court in 'the big game'. He was plowing through traffic on his way down for the winning, last second, lay-up. He glanced up at the clock to gauge his time. You guessed it. He immediately relaxed, slowed down, looked around for his parents in the stands, never getting the shot off. I hope at some point in his life he has found it within himself to forgive me! Knowledge is precious and must be thoughtfully applied.

The late night phone calls. Looking back several things loom as possibilities. They began at about the same time Wayne came into my life – shortly after. It was a time when I was allowing new relationships. I was becoming somewhat more cavalier and less secretive. I am now quite certain there really never were any calls. It doesn't fit the reality of the situation as I have come to understand it. I believe it was a method my mind used to remind me of the terror and whip me back into shape. At that point I not only had my own welfare about which to be concerned but Wayne's as well. The boy was fully innocent and should not be put in harm's way. I needed the nudge to retreat into caution. It took an extreme form that most certainly did terrorize me. Why the form of phone calls? I don't know. I'll leave that for Siggy's followers to ferret out. (Siggy the Ferret – what a great title for a children's' story!)

A little terror. A lot of terror. The Deep Mind has no way of differentiating degree. 'Really' real or 'really' illusion, my terror *was* real – hyperventilating, adrenaline pumping, paranoia inducing, phone call induced terror. It modified my routine. It returned me to the horror of the years just past. I imagine that as I signaled any easing of my vigilance, my DM zapped me again. That is supported by my memory that with each 'call' my reaction increased exponentially. In total there were probably fewer than a dozen such instances – more than enough, however, to keep me in line. (Random, periodic, reinforcement for the behaviorists in the crowd.)

To this day I sometimes awaken to the sound of my phone. Once roused enough to know what's going on, there are no more rings to be heard. The flash of terror is still there but it dissipates and, although I cannot yet smile about it, I can turn over and go back to sleep. It happened just last night. Clearly coming to grips with my ordeal on the conscious level has not depleted its influence at the subconscious level. There will be work to do.

Big Tony in the park. Although it made complete sense at the time, I now understand that Tony in his limo – 600 miles from home – was just a reincarnation of the phone calls. It is unclear to me if it was contained in a dream or if it came in the form of an illusion while I was there in the park. I *could* have seen headlights coming toward me and my mind *could* have used it as an opportunity to inflict a terror-based reminder that I still needed to be careful. Being in the park alone at ten p.m. was certainly *not* being careful. It was just so hard to always be on the lookout, always be suspicious, always be careful, and always put my safety above absolutely everything else. It drained me mentally, physically, and emotionally. It never seemed natural and I took that as a positive sign that my life before Joplin had not always been one of hide and seek – the stakes being my life or that of a loved one.

The only time I really feel the terror anymore is when I contemplate the lost months just prior to Joplin. It wells up in seconds, swirling through my stomach and up into my head. My abdomen becomes heavy and my head pounds and aches. On one occasion a few days ago I threw up. It has all the intensity of all the terror I've known these past years compacted into one small, treacherously volatile package. As I write it has reappeared. My heart pumps and my breathing increases in an erratic tempo as if there is no dependable air supply. I panic – some for a breath and some from the malevolent darkness that is still holed up somewhere deep inside. My interpretation is that those months must have been significantly worse in every possible way than what I experienced from Joplin on. Perhaps it was just that or perhaps there was some secondary trauma that requires that period to remain hidden in the darkness. Why do I even want to know – want to force myself to remember? The answer, I believe, is to purge myself of the last remnants of this *unrelenting darkness*.

I have detailed four images and the associated emotions that recur as stable images even though I have no place for them in my past. I believe they have to be associated with those lost months. If so, and if that yellow motel was in fact one of my very first stops after leaving Wilton, it could be the basis for Candy's motel. In my mind it was lemon drop yellow. Lemon drop. Candy? A stretch but who knows. If my emerging terror continued to the extent I experienced it in my image of being on the bed there, I can understand that my mind might have reduced the motel in size in an attempt to reduce the terror. It might have 'white washed' it as well. All speculation. When I arrived in Joplin my hair was mostly white so if it had been colored – as in the images – at some

170

point I stopped doing that. Had my discomfort lessoned?

Just why my mind insisted on inventing a motel as my first stop in Joplin I don't know. Apparently I remained in a semi-blocked state (for want of a better term) during those first few weeks – there but not entirely there. Perhaps I was wavering between my two realities. Perhaps it was there that my amnesia actually began. I must assume that I either went directly to roach house or did spend some time in a motel or hotel first. Nothing surfaces for me about that. I will assume it was a buffer between past and present. My mind may have been evaluating the wisdom of letting me again have control over my memory. As I say, speculation is all I have.

There are three other images that arrived from *Never, Never Land*. That house with the porch, the sidewalk traversing the gently slope and the bus at the bottom of the hill. The house could be a place I lived post Lemon Drop Motel. I can't add any more features than those that arrived with the first flash – a small, old, two story, place with a porch across the front, several steps up to access it and two front doors probably meaning two apartments. It is not connected in my mind to the sloping sidewalk. As far as I 'really' know the two could have been a continent apart. The bus, however, was connected to the sidewalk image, as was the little college across the street. Why I think it is a college I'm not sure because nothing about that set of memories is really clear.

The image I had much earlier about folding the dollar bill and making sure the 'stop cord' was within easy reach are not specifically attached to the image of the bus at the bottom of the hill. I don't even see me included in that image. Interesting: Of course the stop cord *would* be there. Why would I check and feel such relief upon finding it? My first ride, perhaps? More likely just the generalized anxiety I was feeling about everything. It could have been part of an obsessive/compulsive adjustment tactic. If so, I imagine I checked several time on each and every ride just to make sure it was still there. What a fully uncomfortable – debilitating – way in which to have to live. I wonder where I was going. As I said, I couldn't see myself. Was I wearing that Dairy Queen shirt on my way to work? It is a possibility without any solid verification.

None of the remaining images, which are unattached to place or time, posses even a trace of a pleasant emotion. They are all fear based. I tend to think that lends some credence to the idea that they are representative of those early months of flight. I have been fully unsuccessful in my attempts to regress to that period. In the first place the immediate anxiety becomes debilitating and relaxation is impossible. In the second place all I have to use is *time* – there is no *place* to which I can let my mind drift. Age regression – in this case re-characterized as time regression – works best if there is a known anchor, a place to visualize. (The Deep Mind is image based.) My plan is to use that front porch if I can ever reduce the tension enough to begin.

Last night I induced a deep state of unfocused relaxation. I just let my mind float as if in free association with whatever images, sounds, odors, or feelings came along. My mind cooperated in one way, at least – it remained unfocused. It was a wonderful state of freedom with no tension, worries, or responsibilities. In that sense it was therapeutic. The sole images that lingered in my mind were a holey sock on my foot and a discarded tuna can. I truly do believe that on the label "Charlie" was mooning me. A dirty, worn out sock and a stinking tuna can. Not a whole lot of help Mr. Deep Mind, Sir! Perhaps it has a sense of humor, after all.

It made for some smiles at the time and continues to. Was it saying, "You *can't* get to the *foot* of the w*hole* problem?" Or maybe, "You *can*!" I sincerely doubt it but we psychologist-types often enjoy lingering over such absurdities. (Freudians even believe them!) One of the traits of the DM is to give you something for each request you make. I imagine that on a whim it eenie, meenie, minie, moed up those particular images. If Deep Minds laugh, I'm sure mine was giggling its impish heart out.

In the Elliott Ness dream I believe my DM made its first relatively open attempt at giving up my name. I missed it. Three themes are important. I characterized my sad terror as my darkness. In the dream the flashes from the machine gun lit up the dark alley – my whole darkened world there in the

172

dream. What would it take to *really* light up my inner darkness and drive it away? My name. And what was the name given but once to the gun that was providing that light for me – a *Tommy* gun. Again it may be a stretch but I really don't think so. Think about what was treated in important ways. Did the bullets kill me? Apparently not. Did they even hurt me? Apparently not. Was I arrested? No. Did Ness argue my point of innocence? No. The only significant aspects were the bright, bright, flashes of light that drove away the darkness, and the source of that light – the *Tommy* gun. The name was there. Clearly I wasn't yet ready to receive it.

The Bible and badge guy dream continues to intrigue me. My original fear was that it might indicate my true colors as a bad guy, legitimately being put to death for my crime. I was not disputing the fate. Another, every bit as legitimate interpretation could be that the good guys represented by the Bible and the badge, were unable to punish me suggesting that I had been somehow able to overcome my accusation and prove my innocence. I continued to set things right in the big room arranging and rearranging, cleaning – I'm not sure what else. It may have represented my unfulfilled mission in life to continue 'fixing' things despite apparent overwhelming odds (injection after injection). There had never been a fearful emotion attached to it but rather it was infused with calm and peace and purpose, and a cooperative spirit. As horrendous a picture as it painted, the emotion never reflected it. Also, oddly, perhaps, it has become one of my all-time 'favorite' dreams.

The meaning of the glass objects dream still eludes me. It may have had no real significance. The majority of dreams don't, I believe. They are mostly just the discarding of DM garbage clearing the way for another day. Still, the emotion that flooded the dream when the woman accused me of the theft was overwhelming. My goodness! You know who that woman was? *My wife*, suddenly as clear as can be. It puts an interesting possible twist to the dream (that one I just said was probably insignificant!). Perhaps the glass objects were the lost parts of my life that I was trying to retrieve and collect. The milkiness represented the uncertainty and so on. The rose represented my attempt to control my negative feelings – rage, perhaps – toward her or my situation. Her accusation against me reflected how she most always really had related to me. It represented the fact that I was so sure she would first of all blame me for my disappearance and emphasize the hardship it had visited upon her.

I'm crying. It has never been my intention to hurt her although I doubt if she believes that. My impression was that she delighted in being able to blame me for things – she was, as I recall first of all, a blamer, not a fixer. It helps explain the overwhelming reaction I had to being found at fault by her in the dream. I felt like a little boy caught with my hand in the cookie jar. That is how she always made me feel whenever I did something I wanted to do for myself. I hope those memories of our relationship are false. Certainly something was wrong with it since we decided to live apart.

Interpreted in that way the dream seems to have little to do with my amnesia or flight or my resulting problems. Well, my concern about her reaction to my leaving was there, perhaps. Another interesting thought. My mother's name was Virginia and was called Ginny for short. In my constructed life my wife was named Ginny. Perhaps I harbored the feeling that my wife (in real life) acted like a mother – a disciplinarian, a power figure who could allow and disallow on a whim, the dispenser of guilt, the figure I had to please. Interesting, my fear may have been that my real life wife would have tried to turn my disappearance into a guilt trip for me (while enjoying the role as martyr, herself.). My adolescent personality was partly driven by the 'never be at fault' dictum and some of that may have attached itself to the wife-dynamic in all of this.

Another foible of psychologists – we are given to over-interpreting things.

Remember the bite out of the apple. I doubt if it has reference to the computer company symbol (although if they'd like to divvy up for the publicity I'm providing here, it won't be turned away!!). More likely it was an attempt to tell me to stop the search. It was an attack on my most basic source of inner peace. "Continue and your last connection to sanity will be destroyed – consumed." That, too, may be an overstatement. (Perhaps I had not been appropriately feeding my DM and it just became hungry!!) Or, taking it to an extreme, An apple a day does what? Keeps the doctor away. Devour the apple and maybe the 'doctor' (me) will need to come back. (Perhaps I should consider writing fiction for a living. Oh! I do. Fascinating!)

On a moment to moment basis I still have difficulty keeping my several realities sorted out and kept in their proper places. I am so used to living in my created history that I just slip back into it with no warning. I know it is false, I don't mean I'm slipping back and forth between them at a dissociative level. The problem is exacerbated by the fact that I am still living as Jerry Wilson here in Fayetteville. It is how I am known everywhere. That life story is the one I regularly refer to. I have to be on constant alert to keep it all sorted out in public. Recently, I introduced myself by the wrong name. Throat clearing and coughing with the insertion of the correct name has saved me so far. It is a lot like multi-tasking and as I've proven recently, I am no longer very effective at that. I sign my emails to Carole as Jerry and then have to correct them. I sign mail from the business, Tommy, and hope I catch them all before they zap out into cyber space.

I must get on with contacting my son and brothers. If courage allows, tonight will be the night I make calls. It will be a flip of coin as to whom I will dial first. I've built a case for each one. Bill had been my go to guy most of my adult life. We lived close. He is one of the wisest people I have ever known. We shared psychology as a professional interest. I have been close to his children. He is 79, however, and I don't want to surprise him into a heart attack.

Larry is 77. I guess that is really not much younger. He has lots of support near by – his son, Nevin, if my reconnaissance has been accurate and his fantastic wife Regina. My original plan was to contact him.

There is Bob, of course, my son. I can't put my finger on why, but I feel a great reluctance to contact him and yet it is what I want most of all. I suppose I feel that I hurt him the most – well, not I, but my disappearance. Not only emotional hurt but financial hurt since he and his wife both worked for me (as I recall). They seem to have survived – never any doubt about the two of them making it. Maybe I'll give him the first call. I hope I will do that. I feel like a fifteen year old again, making ready to ask a girl out on my first date. The butterflies have become the huge, prehistoric variety, and their wings are wearing away the lining of my stomach. I feel it churning and sense it bleeding. It is hard to imagine a grown, intelligent, once rather successful man reverting to a blithering teenager in the face of such a simple act. Dial the number and say, "Hello, this is your long lost father."

That's probably really lame. Now, for the rest of the day I'll stew over how to say hello. I just must not let it deter me from calling *somebody*.

7:05 p.m. I surprised myself at how ready I really was to make the call. I waited until after the diner hour and gathered the several numbers beside me on the couch. I sighed deeply, and dialed the number I was very sure was Bob's.

"I'm sorry but that number is no longer in service. . . ."

I must have misdialed. I tried again, very carefully.

"I'm sorry but that number is no longer in service. . . ."

Neurotically, I tried a third time. It seemed the automated operator was getting perturbed at me so I sat the phone down to think. I would try Bill, my oldest brother. It somehow seemed appropriate for him to be number two on my list. That time I was very careful and punched the buttons with precision.

"This is the residence of Ruth and Bill Atherton. We can't come to the phone just now so please leave a message and . . ."

I hung up not thinking it was an appropriate topic for leaving as a phone message. "Hey Bro! This is your kid sib, Tommy boy. What's hap'a'nin', Dude?" It just didn't work. I called twice more at half hour intervals. Still no response. I'd go to the good ol' third try is the charm. Larry.

Carole had done some snooping for me when she was in Jonesboro on a recent jaunt. I had addresses and phone numbers from a current phone book for both Larry and his son, Nevin. I hesitated for only a moment, looking back and

176

forth between the numbers. I poked out Larry's. Ring! Ring!! Ring!!!

"Hello."

I swallowed hard.

"Is Larry Atherton there?"

I took a deep breath.

"This is Larry Atherton."

There was a short pause on my end.

"The Larry Atherton from Carson, Illinois."

"Yes."

"This is your brother Tom."

"Tom! Gina, it's Tom!"

The conversation lasted a half hour – maybe more. I gave him the short, short version of my situation promising that a longer written epistle would follow. He filled me in on the state of life (and death – my wife Pat, and Dad's wife, Dorothy had both died.) Unbelievably, my father is alive and very well at 102! I got brought up to date on the major things with promises of much more when we got together – we will make it soon.

Then, coincidence of all coincidences, the following day my father was moving from one assisted living residence to another (a twenty minute drive for me) and my brother Bill and his wife Ruth were in the area to assist with the undertaking (The reason they did not answer their phone.) I couldn't believe it. Well, I could, but you will understand. Larry had intended to be there as well but his wife, Regina, had fallen and hurt her hip and the trip looked just too long under those conditions. Without the fall and their delayed trip plans, that phone call number three would have fallen silent as well. Regina is convinced it's fate or something similar. I won't dispute it as a possibility.

I got phone numbers of the two rest homes and called Carole – good ol', always ready for adventure or consolation, Carole – and she offered her services for the day so I could reunite with my family. I slept no more than two hours that night but seemed bright eyed and bushy tailed throughout the next day. (My adrenal glands screamed out for mercy.) Not knowing that Larry would reach them by phone and inform them of my pending presence – which was a very good idea – I arrived to open arms. Bill took a few minutes to prepare my dad. We didn't know how he might react and didn't want to upset him.

He was immediately – I mean IMMEDIATELY – ready and a few minutes later I entered his room. He looked like dad. He sounded like dad. Most of all he smiled and hugged like dad. He, Bill, Ruth, Carole and I talked for several hours. We remembered, we laughed, we filled the room with love. I am dumbfounded about the way I remembered things – infinitesimal things that I probably hadn't even thought about for years before I disappeared. They rolled off my tongue. Bill or Dad would bring something up and I would remember. I remembered the dresser in Dad's room and had stories about getting in trouble for flipping the metal drawer pulls to hear the raucous noise. Where had all of those memories been? It is hard to imagine how much mental energy must have been expended in order to keep them suppressed. How did I have any left over to support my minute to minute functioning? Perhaps mental energy is like love – it comes in a never ending supply.

Dad is fantastic for 102. Heck, he's fantastic for 82. He walks a mile every day, eats pretty much what he wants to, and is loved by everybody who knows him. He delivers the mail to the rooms and participates in a variety of helping activities. He is going to miss his place but legal issues arose within management and the doors were closed.

We left dad for his lunch and a nap while the other four of us went out to eat. We returned for a second brief visit and then went our separate ways – Bill and Ruth back to Illinois and Carole and I back to Fayetteville.

I still have to contact Bob. I discovered that for several months he and Abby have been living in Normal, Illinois within a few miles of Bill and Ruth. The others refrained from calling him about me, thinking the 'word' should come from my mouth. I'd have been happy for them to have been a bit less proper and get me off the hook for that first contact but I knew it should be my responsibility. I tried his correct phone number while at Dad's but again was met by the answering machine. I will try again tonight. There is still apprehension in my bones but everything else has worked out so well, I am going to believe that will, too. I will watch the news and wait again for 7:05. For some reason(s) this is suddenly a tremendously big deal. I'll eat. (That *is* the appropriate response to debilitating, gut churning, I'll-probably-throw-up, anxiety, isn't it?)

I will go into more detail later about things I have learned through all of this and in what senses it has benefited me but one thing is for sure: I can face the most terrifying situations and come out relatively unscathed. Carole calls it courage. I'm not sure what to call it. Is it courageous to pursue the only option one has? I was never a quitter. It has seldom been an option that I considered. When plan 'A' failed I was fully confident that I would find plans 'B' through 'ZZ' if that became necessary in order to make 'whatever' work. As a boy I would often begin projects for which I knew I didn't possess the skill or knowledge to finish. I would learn the skill or acquire the knowledge at the moment plan met ignorance or ineptness. In fact, I grew to enjoy those times because I could feel them pushing me beyond what I had been.

When I was a little boy dad would seldom come right out and answer my, "How can I," questions. He'd point to something relevant or he'd say, "Could that (pointing) help?" I loved those moments because it proved he had confidence in me. His little direction providers were a million times more helpful than would have been direct answers or demonstrations. I suspect that contributes to how I have come to relish developing mysteries. Develop an impossible mission and then complete it. What fun!

Throughout these 19 years I have seldom dwelled on the long term negative effect the experience might have on me. I always ate. I always had clothing. I always had a sheltered place in which to sleep. I always had people to do for. I always had what I needed, and what I *needed* grew to become all that I *wanted*. That may be the grandest lesson I have learned.

I have tried calling Bob three times since I arrived home. Still the recording. I will try again later on.

. . . .

Still the recording. Later. I hope they aren't answering because they see Jerry Wilson on the caller ID and, not knowing that person, they let it go. I'll continue trying up until bedtime then consider changing my approach tomorrow.

I waited until 8:30 the following morning and dialed the number still another time. A man's voice answered.

"Hello."

"Bob?"

"Yes."

"This is your father," (or some such words. I really don't remember. My intention was solely to break the news.).

The conversation went on for thirty minutes. It was cordial with no discernable trace of emotion over the phone – matter of fact from the 'yes' to the 'good-by'. On the other hand it was an emotional rush for me. It was wonderful. I don't think I actually recognized Bob's voice but his vocabulary and unique phrases let me know I had the right person. I explained my situation and referred to it as amnesia. He said, "You mean fugue." About one in a million people understand that concept. I wasn't at all surprised that he did. Like his father, Bob always enjoyed learning about the esoteric, obscure, obtuse if you will. As a grade schooler he'd fly through his regular work so he could get to the extra credit work, which meant he could explore 'far out' areas of knowledge – the truly important stuff. We once joked that between the two of use we probably harbored more useless knowledge than any thousand other people you could gather together. For most folks that would probably seem senseless. For us it was a badge of some kind – positive and maybe even a little arrogant (as I recall).

His life seems to be good although the words that conveyed that were not backed up with the usual tone or emotion. He said that he had taught writing in a Junior College for five or so years but only after I mentioned Larry had indicated that to me. I heard little else about his career. There are no children. He seemed somewhat guarded about personal matters – unwilling to have his place in the world known by the great-unwashed-public. He mentioned that he

180

had been in a serious train wreck a number of years ago but did not elaborate. Bill had given me a few details at his wife's urging. I really don't understand the full ramifications but clearly some remain.

Regardless of anything else, it was the absolute highlight of my past twenty years. I've relived the conversation word by word searching for feelings and implications. I know I should just let it be and accept it at face value. That's hard to do when it's all I have from the past 20 years. I will try, however. Whatever he is, and however he is I love him with all my heart. It is all fine. My need to be with him grows by the minute. I told him I would email him a summary of my experiences. We will talk again after that. I am as high as I've ever been. I need to take a walk and dissipate this adrenalin.

There are so many possibilities in my life all of a sudden. I'm not used to having positive possibilities – at least not those which I can truly consider pursuing without the fear of dreadful consequences for myself or others. I can stay here like I am with the wonderful added dimension of having found my family allowing my happy, warm, loving, circle to be extended. I can move to lots of places – in or near to Larry and Regina. I can move up the road twenty miles to be within walking distance of my father. I can move back to the Illinois area to be close to Bob and Bill. I can move to Timbuktu for goodness sake and dance the Timbuk in my Tutu. I could even roam around from relative to relative – purchase an RV perhaps so I would be less of an inconvenience. (Probably no money for an RV unless I can make my passion for writing pay off.)

How do I react to other options? I don't want to engage in therapy anymore. I could really enjoy teaching. I love sessions in which folks pick my brain – therapeutic techniques, writing, parenting, value exploration, and things like that. I could easily spend large amounts of time doing clay sculpture. My products are not good enough to bring in sufficient money to live on. I love crafts and building. I fantasize about finding a big open building that I could remodel into a single big living space – preferably one up high

181

enough so I could enjoy looking out over these beautiful Ozark Mountains or grand views elsewhere. I love being in situations where I can model my positive social philosophy. Most of all, I guess, I love writing.

I know I'm no super hot pen. What I write isn't going to win awards. Big publishing houses are most likely not going to pick up my books. I'm sure I'll never meet Oprah in person. That's all okay. I write because I love to write. Wouldn't it be the grandest of all hoots to write with Bob!! (That was not really a question.)

Back in the days when I had to keep a low profile it was impossible to consider promoting my books on radio or television. That's not a barrier anymore. Interesting! This is the first time I've considered that possibility. The 'ham' in me likes that idea. It is hard to comprehend this new freedom and the possibilities it offers.

CHAPTER TEN
The Brightening: Useful things I've learned

For years I have admonished my patients and young friends to always find something useful to take away from every encounter, 'good or bad'. I therefore feel compelled to undertake that same mission at this juncture in my life. What useful things have I learned?

> The accumulation of stuff is fully unimportant. It contributes in no way to improving the lot and longevity of mankind and *that* seems to have become my mission. I've spent time doing meticulous inventories of what middle class people have. My conclusion is that only about 30% is needed, and of that at least half is far more expensive than it needs to be. I can only guess at the percentage for the wealthy. One percent perhaps – one tenth of one percent? And yet there are sick, hungry, abused children in every city in our country.

> When the blaming/punishing mentality (approach to problems) is replaced by the analyze/fix mentality, life immediately gets better for everybody involved (and often for those not immediately involved). Education and training outperform punishment virtually every time. During these past nineteen years, I have seen it proved over and over and over again. How is it that mankind so doggedly refuses to accept and embrace that? The evidence has been in for hundreds of years and still we build prisons instead of schools we cut after school programs for kids in order to fund more

183

juvenile cops on the streets.

> Although it wasn't a new concept to me, I certainly proved to myself that there are good people everywhere. Present yourself as a kind and helpful person and good people come out of the walls. They are everywhere. I found the opposite to also be true. Present yourself as a jerk, a people user, untrustworthy, and you are soon isolated (at least by intelligent, thoughtful, people). I watched it happen to others every day. Comfortable people are included. Uncomfortable people are excluded (unless they are tough enough to intrude).

It is not a rocket science concept although a significant percent of our population miss it. Their neighborhoods if not their homes, teach that being nice is soft and disgraceful. To get ahead in the world and be respected you have to be tough and take what you want. Their work ethic is quite the opposite of everything it needs to be in order to succeed in mainstream society. They misinterpret being *feared* for being *respected* – not a new take on it but when you live elbow to elbow with it day in and day out its effects gain clear focus. My heart goes out to the unfortunate kids who grow up in such situations and therefore must base their own social philosophy on it. When you don't dare be nice to outsiders because that shows you are weak (unacceptable) and when trying to be frightening to gain respect clearly isn't working very well (there is always somebody more frightening and powerful than you), there are no alternatives. Well, there is the one and that is to kowtow to the most frightening person around, do his bidding without question, and live in fear of him and *his* enemies forever. In essence I lived that way for nineteen years. The situation was only different in degree. I can see how rage develops and boils over. I can see how self-worth comes to be defined solely in terms of how tough you are. I can see how helplessness and hopelessness develop and soon come to rule your life.

A sad turn in all of that is that back when I first entered that world it was only the *guys* who were immediately sucked into that hurtful, humanity ending, philosophy and way of life. Today a significant percent of *girls* are living that life as well. And, it is no longer confined to the poorer 'class'. Middle and

184

upper class kids are now defining their worth by their toughness – by their ability to keep others under their thumb through terror tactics. These kids from middle class and well-moneyied families often seem to be less concerned with extending their own power than in just terrorizing others they don't even really know. It is frightening. Why do I mention the girls? Because today – especially among the poor – it is the women who raise the children – Period! End of Story. Back when most females modeled the softer philosophy in homes, children at least had some chance of avoiding the hate/power based approach to living. An alternative was present. But now? With violence projected everywhere in our society today, I suppose I should not be surprised. As I said, there are still good, loving, inclusive, non-violent people everywhere. I have to take my solace in that I suppose. It would be easier if I felt there were some concerted, grass-root effort to counteract the philosophy of violence with one of love and logic and common sense as the long term survival of the species is given universal consideration.

> There are people in need, everywhere. This situation causes some inner conflicts for me. I have come to define myself as a people-tender. I take care of folks. It has become a rather selfish need deep inside me to have people around who need my care. I have to be mindful that my mission is to help fix and set free, rather than to find and make others dependent on me. I have seen that latter tendency lessen since Wayne came into my life. Perhaps it is related to my fear of losing my loved ones again. What I have learned is that when you help somebody fix himself, you exchange parts of yourselves, and therefore carry the other person with you forever. There is no loss. There is only gain. Again, my experience with our foster boys taught me that early on, but insights not regularly practiced tend to fall by the wayside (get stored in cobweb covered cubby holes in the furthest recesses of the Deep Mind.)

I suppose the disheartening lesson I learned regarding the ubiquitous needy is that most of those who are *less* needy find ways of making the truly needy vanish. For some I imagine it is to protect themselves from having to share in the

185

misery. For others it is to assuage their guilt over allowing such a social blight to happen. Some just want it to go away so they don't have to be involved. Many, all quite selfishly, don't want to use any significant portion of their own resources to assist those who are in need. Their consciousness merely redefines them as *needy* rather than *human*. In further support of their position they tend to blame the needy for being needy. "It was her doing, not mine, that set her and her four kids out there on the street, homeless."

More and more I hear both middle of the road and conservative ministers preaching how right it is for their parishioners to amass and enjoy the comforts of great wealth and suffer no pangs of guilt about keeping it just for themselves (so long as they tithe to the church which, more and more is used for buildings and ministers' salaries than 'good works'). I'm not a bible thumping Christian but I do know the scriptures and am ashamed of my fellow men (from any religion) that purport to live by their 'good book' and yet find it so easy to overlook the core teaching presented there – love. When one believes in the preciousness of mankind there can be only one social agenda – we must take good care of each other and prepare our planet to provide well for the needs of the next generations.

I have found little genuine, put-your-money-and-services-where-your-mouth-is, man-on-the-street, support for my contention that mankind is precious and that we each have a significant responsibility for the welfare of others. Interestingly, and yet understandably I suppose, the helpfulness ethic is present to a far greater degree among the needy themselves than it is among the less needy and affluent. The homeless man will share his can of soup with the passerby but the man in the three hundred dollar suit won't toss him a quarter. It has not been a really positive finding overall, I suppose, but it has supported my contention that I must continue fighting the good battle here.

I am absolutely appreciative of the billons of dollars a few of the wealthiest people in the western world are giving to humanitarian causes. They won't gain my full respect, however, until they start living in the apartment next door to me on the $750.00 a month personal budget I allow myself.

> I'm not a Mother Teresa. I make no pretense in that direction. I have stuff well beyond what I need. I have four rooms when I could certainly get by with one. I have a few bucks put back for another rainy day. I eat out sometimes when I could just as well eat in. I have ten shirts when goodness knows I don't need that many. I have eight sweaters accumulated over the nineteen years. Who could possibly need eight sweaters? I've even been known to buy new shoes before the soles have worn through on my old ones. I live very, very, well, you see. Just think of the Eden we could create if we all chose to live as well as I do. My point: I am so thankful that these years have helped me sort out the truly important things in life from the *absolutely* unimportant. People are important. Stuff, status, and wealth, are unimportant.

Enough (probably toooooooo much) sermonizing. One final note: When I was back in college I was offended that so many of the people there only did good works to assure themselves a place in Heaven. I used to think we didn't need help from folks working from that kind of totally selfish motivation. I've given that up and gladly welcome charitable help and funds from any source regardless of the self-centered motivation. I'm sorry so many of them miss out on the true joy only accessible in all of the known universe to us humans, but I try to work on that with them as I can. Dad taught me to be a good model of what I believed in. Everyday I try to be that model and encourage others to do the same. Interestingly, I suppose, we all *do* model what we believe deep inside, don't we. What others see us doing becomes our bumper sticker for life.

> Lest I leave a fully depressing picture of what my recent life has taught me about man's selfishness, I *have* found people who are willing to help people, everywhere I've been. I knew an 18 year old recovering drug addict who, after work at the restaurant most nights, would buy two take out meals and set them on the dumpster for the homeless men in the neighborhood. He didn't humiliate them by sticking around to gloat over and be acknowledged for his generosity. He'd been

one of them once. He knew how it was. It was his turn – his grand opportunity – to help those in need.

There was one point in my darkened life when I had but twenty-five dollars to my name – a position I had been promised fell through. In desperation, I found a job in an ice cream store and when I opened my wallet to hand the owner my identification card she noticed there was no money inside. She tried to remain nonchalant about it all and said, "Sometimes we pay by the day for new employees if that will help them out during the first two weeks." I accepted her generous, kind, human-friendly offer and allowed myself to eat that evening for the first time in several days. There were kind and helpful, generous people everywhere I went. (I remember that event in crystal clear images although I don't know the when or where of it. Most likely during those first 32 months that still elude me. No other memories have followed me from that place of employment. Her loving kindness has pierced my darkness if only for a moment. Thank you, whoever you were.)

> Focusing on the needs of others, though not reducing my terror, kept life in perspective. I don't recall ever believing that I was worse off than everybody else, but even if I had, I would not have been able to ignore the plights of others. In my fantasy about my childhood, the story went that ten percent of whatever we earned went into our 'Help Jar' and was used to assist those who needed it more than we did. Remember, we were by far the poorest family in town, but still, where we saw need we did what we could to fix it. I can see, now, that reflected the reality of my 'real' home. My parents took in kids who needed a place and they became like family. Our church was a benevolent bee hive. The women made quilts and soap to send to France during WWII and to Germany afterwards. We cleaned the homes of the old or infirmed. We did without sugar in our home so we could slip packets of it in among the quilts. We had a food bank long before they were called food banks. Mom always fed the 'tramps' that walked our alley on their ways to nowhere. My two realities were really quite similar in tone and philosophy even if not in geography, structure, or 'personal'.

My point is that I've learned that I possess a well-modeled, well-tutored drive to be helpful. That need didn't seem to wane throughout my 'away time'. In fact, I believe it increased in power, perhaps to counter my own sense of helplessness driven by the disconcerting reality I was experiencing around me everyday. Most certainly I understand it better now. I appreciate it more now. I am more thoughtful and systematic in its application now. Those are, I believe, all good things that have come about. Would they have come about anyway? I don't know. Back then I was working too hard, too long, seven days a week, month after month. I remember how exhausted I was all the time running on three and four hours of sleep a night. It had gone on for years. Being able to find time for more helpfulness would have been impossible. Of course, many of the folks I saw were seen gratis. I suppose that counts. Even though I can't know what might have been I'll put this growth in the plus column, here.

> I believe behavior, which is not an inborn possibility, can never be effectively fostered. Put another way, if a behavior potential doesn't preexist within us it can't be developed and put on autopilot. It follows, therefore, (perhaps in a round-about fashion) that we have a human potential for mutual helpfulness that just needs to be modeled and nurtured. It goes without saying that we have the potential for the opposite – complete selfishness. Developmentally it necessarily blossoms on its own in young children. "Mine!" "No!" "Hit me kid and I'll knock you on your keester!" It requires deliberate, thoughtful training and modeling with positive feedback to overcome those, biologically necessary, self-protective tendencies, and they must be tempered with consistently altruistic, socially positive traits.

Thoughtful parenting based on verifiable knowledge: I virtually *never* saw it happening. What I saw were parents inventing the parenting wheel all over again with no apparent conception that there were really helpful, proven, fact-based, procedures and information readily available. What I saw were parents surrendering the lives of their children to child-raising procedures based on fully unfounded opinion and, mostly, on inconsistent whim. I have become convinced the only way to assure the comfortable survival of the human species is by way of a loved-based, fix-it don't blame-it, inclusive, altruistic, approach to parenting.

That is not to say I was completely successful in accomplishing that in my own home and for that I am forever distressed. It's one thing to understand that at any given moment a person can only do as well as that person can do. It is often far more difficult to live with it in retrospect. I found it difficult to balance the needs of others with the needs of my family. Things I assumed were being handled appropriately at home were not and I should have not assumed they were. I abdicated responsibility that should have never been handed off. I regret that. Perhaps Mother Nature has played a vicious trick on us as a species. She only allows wisdom to bloom as the results of mistakes well taken. On the other hand, perhaps she envisioned us living in multi-generational villages in which case wisdom would always be close at hand. It is a wonder that the first, practice kids, in a family ever survive emotionally. In my case I was fortunate. My parents learned well from whatever early mistakes they might have made with my two older siblings. By number three they were ready to do a very good job, I think. (Says the man who just spent nineteen years in emotional limbo. Hmmm? At least I thought I was having a mostly great childhood and adolescence. Reality! What a deceptive and cumbersome concept!)

I sound bitter, disillusioned, and pessimistic. My entire adult life has been inundated with cases involving the sad results of inappropriate parenting. It was my 'therapeutic purpose' to confront that and 'fix' it to whatever degree was possible. *I* understand that it is really not all that difficult to raise well-adjusted, socially positive, kids. In that knowledge I am extremely positive and optimistic that it can happen. I must say it galls me that our public education system abdicates all responsibility to systematically teach the truly most important subjects – mental health, social responsibility, parenting, building and maintaining positive interpersonal relationships. We don't even teach driver education anymore.

190

By one estimate I've heard *that* alone may account for as many as 10,000 deaths annually. Do kids die because they don't have second year algebra? Do they die and kill other innocents because they don't know about the Punic Wars? More and more each year the public education system seems to be leaving the human needs of its students behind in favor of higher SAT scores. Did I say it galls me? I talk with students almost every week – informally, here and there. I am appalled at how much they don't know and how much of what they do know they don't understand. The one-room school house was clearly superior in many ways. I remember my son and I often spoke about that. We might have even made plans in the direction of reinstituting such settings. I will now cease and desist.

> What else have I learned? When I was a boy and I would make something or fix something or do something, folks would ask, "Where did you learn how to do that?" I always thought it was a really dumb question because I just thought up how to do it. Nobody had showed me. It was as if they did not allow for common sense or creativity in a kid's being.

I have to give my upbringing high marks in terms of fostering my creativity and it has stood me in good stead throughout all these years. While 'away', I never once came up against a problem I was unable to solve or work my way around – at least not on days when I had the determination and energy to keep things fixed. My parents always let me try even when they understood I might not succeed. That was fine. Protecting me from failure would have been a terrible mistake. It gave me the chance to rethink things and better assess my potential for success going in. I learned my limits and my skill levels. From that grew my ability to innovate my survival. I had to be sly, creative, patient, reserved, resourceful, careful, self-sufficient, alert, analytic, and on down a long list of descriptors important in maintaining one's life within the most fragile of circumstances. I am sure that my intelligence played a part but in the end it had more to do with common sense and creativity than anything else. Common sense only develops when you are encouraged and allowed to try (and fail) in a non-blame based setting.

Whenever I met a new challenge the necessary skill just seemed to tumble out of me and arrive mostly full blown in the moment. I needed to do electrical wiring – I knew just how to do it. I needed to reweave tears in pants – I knew just how to do it. I needed to tutor kids in physics, or English, or the bookwork side of auto mechanics – I knew just how to do it. I needed to write a musical for a junior high – I knew just how to do it. I needed to capture the imaginations of the recalcitrant kids in a class of 'educationally handicapped' freshmen – I knew just how to do it. I decided to do clay sculpture – I knew just how to do it. I could not have possibly been trained to do all of the things I did, and yet they all seemed so natural. It was as though I were the reincarnation of the Great Impostor. If I wanted to do something, I could not only do it but typically I could do it better than most. It elevated my sense of worth and my feeling of value. It offered me a safety factor of a kind. It grew from the fertile kernel my folks allowed and nurtured.

> It is no great revelation. William James, the late philosopher and psychologist, pretty well handled it way back when. Still, I had to experience it to truly understand it. *Reality* is not a something, not a given that we all share. Reality is strictly a personal interpretation. It is what one believes it to be at any given moment.

It goes further than that, I found, Dr. James. Things going on in our 'reality of the present' can, and in fact are, affected by and even driven by the 'reality not present'. In the first instance, I truly believed the constructed past I developed through self hypnosis. It *was* my reality and I held virtually no doubt about it. (I'm never a 100% guy!) In the second instance, the reality that had been mine prior to my 'disappearance' remained a powerful influence in my mind. It poked through on numerous instances and freely populated my writing and my dream life. It was as if I had one reality guiding my day to day functioning and a separate one (unknown to me) managing a large part of my Deep Mind. It appears that hidden reality had the power to 'surface' and yet not be known to the JerryMe as it did such things as order a birth certificate and marriage license and school transcript – for what reason I – the present day incarnation of the TommyMe – still have no idea. It was able to write and receive mail. It was able to buy and install a lockbox and put my 'old' name – Tom Atherton – on my mailbox (right along side Jerry's name and the name of my publishing company). JerryMe never saw that name, he never saw the lockbox, he never saw the key to the lockbox on his key ring. If I am that Tommy who was surfacing from time to time I now have no memory of it. How can I construe this? The forgotten Tommy in Jerry's amnesia is now itself amnesic about its own previous presence and activities during Jerry's life with amnesia. (I suppose some resourceful person out there will be able to diagram that!)

So what was it again that I learned about reality? It is, at best, a momentary rendering of one's probable situation impinged upon and adjusted by forces we will probably never even know are active. (Quantum physics meets Tom and Jerry!) I take most things less seriously, now. I see most things as tentative. I approach 'verified' knowledge as less substantial, less forever, less the bottom line. What is, *is*, for the moment, most likely, perhaps, I assume, you think?

> What else? It has been implied before, but my confidence in myself has grown immensely. Every single night as I prepared for bed I told myself I had successfully navigated one more day. I had done what it took. I had succeeded. I had handled all challenges. I was better prepared now for tomorrow. Most nights I even believed all of that.

Interestingly, the continued terror appeared to strengthen my self-confidence. It became a contest – me against the terror – and every single evening I could claim victory. I likened it to how a victorious gladiator must have felt when he returned alive to his bedding one more night. He knew he would have to fight tomorrow but he gained confidence from his success today.

Still, I cried myself to sleep every single night for nineteen years. It was less about the terror in my life and more about my loss and loneliness – my uncertainty – my darkness.

193

> I developed an unorthodox approach to writing. It involved putting a main character into a setting with just the glimmer of an end goal in sight. I then sat back and watched the plot develop as I put my fingers to the keys. Characters were added as needed. Action followed naturally as it was required to work the story on to the end. I came to call it the Milieu Method – named only because people kept asking me what method I used, so I invented the term for ease of communication (as if all words have not been invented for that same purpose!). (*Milieu: an exciting approach to writing*, 2007.)

The method mimicked my life. I was a character in a situation. My goal was survival – there were secondary goals along the way of course – and I added other 'characters' to my life as became necessary. In the end, I hoped to find the lost me and not knowing how I was going to do that I just kept trying things. I think it works very well in crafting a story. Evidently it worked well in finding myself.

> I also learned that I am a nice guy. I have held myself to the strictest scrutiny for nineteen years and I feel not so much as one fiber of my being that suggests otherwise. People like me. That, of course, helps prove my point – I'm a nice guy. My first inclination is always to help and fix. I just never enter a problem or scene trying to determine blame, which inevitably is followed by the imposition of punishment. I first ask, "What needs to be fixed?" Then, "How can I help fix it?"

It was how I had to live my own life all those years. Allowing myself to be trapped in the idea that I might have done some heinous thing and therefore should just stand by, willingly taking my punishment – amnesia, loneliness, despair – would get me nowhere. Early on (at least from Joplin on) I decided to fix things. I won't say that there were never doubts about the final outcome of my 'time out', but those periods always soon passed. Even during the time I was depressed I didn't really ever throw in the towel. There was some base-line strength even then. My depression was more like a temporary vacation from the fight, the responsibility, and the unrelenting terror.

Were there times when I would have probably sold my very life in order to know, once and for all, what it was all about? Yes, there were. But in general, I was determined to stay the course and fix things.

> Early on I came to understand that I possessed a positive work ethic. When I was sweeping floors (I know I did that but can't remember where or when or under what circumstances) I was determined to be the best floor sweeper in the state. When I washed dishes, mine had to be cleaner than they had ever been before. Whatever it was, I worked to do the best I could do. I'd invent new ways to accomplish routine tasks in a superior manner – faster, more thorough, more complete. I would chuckle to myself when my co-workers would watch with admiration and ask, "Who taught you how to do that?" I was six years old again looking into the adult face of infertile intellect. I'd answer, "Oh, a guy I once worked with." Unbelievably, that was consistently satisfactory. Thanks again, Mom and Dad.

I assume I worked as diligently back when I was doing therapy. It is hard to think of a task that requires any higher degree of mental precision and ethic. I remember many sleepless nights back then as I worried over doing this or doing that for someone. Should I take this tack in treatment or should I take that? How long should I continue on this path before I try some other? Should I try some new, unconventional approach that might be frowned upon by my overly cautious, less innovative, colleagues? The struggle was never ending. It was a constant drain on my being.

> Something that was long in coming was my ability to love – that is not the correct way to state it. It was not my ability to love. It was my willingness to get close enough to others to allow them to become the objects of my love. Wayne was the first. Perhaps Carole the second. I've written about the conflict Wayne presented. He just arrived in my life doggedly determined to remain a part of it. I couldn't bring myself to refuse him. I soon understood how much I needed somebody. I agonized over my high selfishness quotient. Perhaps it should have been another adult but what was, *was*. I weighed the risks of the possible harm that might come to

195

him from being close to me with the clear harm he would experience from being rejected by me. I listed the probable positives and in the end allowed it to happen.

I had always been deeply involved in the lives of others and I was suddenly without anybody. It left a huge black hole inside me that sucked at my spirit. (I recognized that early on, while I was living in the roach house.) In the beginning, I believe, I clearly felt the need for Wayne more than he felt the need for me. I was an oddity in his world and he just wanted to check me out. Later on I believe that evened out. It was somehow safer with a youngster than with an adult. [My son astutely pointed out to me, recently, that my life was always so involved with kids that I really never had time to cultivate an adult friend. He appeared (to me) to be overjoyed when he heard Carole was a part of my life.] Wayne and I have been very good for each other – we continue to be very good for each other.

> I am relearning about romance – or at least the possibility of romance. For 19 years, out of loyalty to my deceased wife (in the fantasy *that was* my reality) I did not let myself become 'involved' with another woman. The fact that a constant state of terror tends to diminish ones sexual urges undoubtedly worked in concert with that misplaced faithfulness to allow my unquestioned celibacy. Since my 'awakening' and the more realistic perception that came with it, my required monk-like days have passed insomuch as I regularly and guiltlessly enjoy looking at women and being in their company and thinking about something more. In some ways I feel fifteen again – as if these feelings are all new and rushing in on me with reckless abandon. How terrible. How wonderful. How in the world does a fifteen year old possibly handle it?

> There is still more for me to learn. I find myself awakening during the night with . . . how can I characterize it . . . flashes of images that fall into that growing category I think of as 'disconnected pieces'. I hope they will someday fall into place and assemble that lost period in my life. The list is becoming sizeable. I've recently seen a shelter on a high rooftop – two doors angled against a huge air vent and covered

196

in a black, plastic, tarp. There are things inside – not sure what, a mattress I believe. Could it have been my home for a while? I see a man, myself I'm pretty sure, cleaning himself up in the restroom of a church – as if it were a regular routine. I'm not in rags but close to it. It's clearly summertime somewhere in the south. I see myself selling papers in a bus station – city buses it seems. Could that help account for my comforted reaction to the smell of diesel during the Greyhound trip? I see myself making caramel corn in big, copper, vats – maybe at a store in a mall. There are more bus riding visions and Thanksgiving dinner at the table of an unrecognized family.

There is nothing yet that assigns those visions to time or place. None carry pleasant emotions. They are all edged in fear and helplessness. I can see the busses but I can't read the signs that grace their bellies. I can see the church but I can't read the inscription above its door. I see myself in a library – one different from Joplin or Fayetteville. I am reading or maybe I'm writing – the image is blurred.

What I have learned is that there are bits and pieces – puzzle pieces – showing themselves from time to time. I will continue to collect them and spread them out on the table waiting for the final configuration to appear. I can reasonably predict but one aspect of that final depiction – it will be simply terrifying!

I am coming to believe that my mind truly does know best. I need a long rest from all that is frightening, terror-ridden, mentally exhausting, and defined by my helplessness. Good boy, Deep Mind. Good boy!

In the meantime I am going to move forward with my life. It won't really be a new life; it will be a melding of what I have had these past years here in Fayetteville, and those elements from before that can enhance and extend it. That will mostly be family and legitimate memories, I believe. There is no life left for me back in my before. There are some extensions from it – my incredibly wise, insightful, and knowledgeable son, for beginners. He amazes me. My other family members and their unconditional acceptance. Waves of love like I can not remember before. The close proximity to my father – twenty minutes up the road. How absolutely wonderful is that – all of that!

I abandoned my world of safety. I survived a world of terror. I learned many wonderful things about myself. I feel stronger than ever before. I'm back – well, mostly. There are loved ones reaching out to me – old and new. My dear father requires no explanation, accepts me back without reservation, and continues to offer me his love – it never stopped, of course. His wonderful smile and ever gentle hugs that now greet me as I enter his room make it worth every moment, every fright, every tear that I had to endure as I battled back out of my Unrelenting Darkness.

The end (well, hopefully, not quite.)

OTHER BOOKS
By Thomas D. Atherton
writing under various pennames.

The David Lawrence Trilogy - Gary Hutchison

The Box: A professor and his nephew race against time to defuse six biotoxin bombs placed by a madman in six locations around the world. The box hold the only clues. An exploration of philosophic positions regarding the reestablishment and maintenance of Planetary Health. 1-885631-99-5

The Strap: Professor Lawrence and Kit find themselves globetrotting to rescue Ari's kidnapped son and return him safely to his home. More cryptic clues, adventure and philosophic jousting. 1-885631-88-X

The Map: (Best read between the other two) The Professor and Kit are off to claim the treasure they found in Brazil (The Box). Rather than a weekend outing it becomes a life threatening search with Pirates, natural disasters, and more. 1-885631-74-X

RECENT RELEASES

Deep Down Forever Happiness: Gary Hutchison
A manual for the *I'm not as happy as I'd like to be.* One basic change in a person's approach to living is all it takes to make the difference – forever. The author's tried and true approach. **ISBN: 1-885631-91-X**

Ripples Gary Hutchison
A wise old man stumbles onto a needy fourteen year old runaway. Their conversations run the gambit of life's important topics. They change each others lives forever. **ISBN: 1-885631-57-X**

My Unrelenting Darkness Thomas D Atherton
Most people awaken each morning to a flood of memories. We know our name, our history, the members of our family, what we do for a living, what sort of person we are, our favorite colors and foods, and down a long list of the familiar. Not so for Jerry Wilson. Each morning for 19 years he awoke to but two certainties: His name was not really Jerry Wilson and the terror, which had been his for years, would begin all over again right from where it had left him the night before.

MYSTERIES

Sanity in search of Peter Alexander
Garrison Flint

Peter Alexander - a kind, soft spoken, bookstore manager and writer - awakens to realize the week just past has been erased from his memory. A blackmail note suggests that he was videotaped killing someone. During the following ten days he records in a journal his every thought and emotional reaction as he plays cat and mouse with the note writer - an anonymous vigilante bent on killing him. The book presents the struggle, questions, terror and even humor that arise within his mind as he searches for answers while, in his words, *"I am moving closer and closer to that point of no return where one silently slips seamlessly from sanity into madness."* ISBN: 1-885631-73-1

Red Grass at Twilight: A suspense mystery -
Garrison Flint

A bright, mild-mannered, middle aged man struggles to regain his memory while being forced to evade ugly adversaries who seem determined to stop him before that can occur. Why are so many people pursuing him? He is not at all certain which side of the law his antagonists are on and that leaves his own position in doubt - good guy or bad guy? Because of that uncertainty, he can't engage the help of the police. From the opening page in which he "emerges from a dark cloud of nothingness" possessing only two bags and an all-encompassing sense of foreboding, to the final, nail-biting, terrifying scene high atop a hotel roof, the reader is kept guessing. ISBN:1-885631-40-5

The Raymond Masters Mystery Series
(Adult and young adult)
Garrison Flint

The Murder No One Committed: A Raymond Masters Mystery

While consulting with a noted writer as she prepares her newest book, Raymond Masters, a retired criminal investigator is confronted with her murder. The writer had been openly hated by those who worked for her and each suspect harbors more than enough motive to want her dead. The more clues he uncovers, the more obvious becomes his conclusion: "This is a murder no one committed." (He solves it, of course! Can you beat him to discovering the unusual twist this case presents?)

The Case of the Smiling Corpse: A Raymond Masters Mystery -

Masters is asked to assist the home town police solve the murder of a retired banker. Was it the teen age boy whose car had killed the banker's wife; the waitress at the local café with a special interest in the handyman who, it turns out, is handy with things others than tools; the sister-in-law who may inherit the victim's estate; or a hit man hired by his wife before she was killed? Initially, it looks like suicide as the body is found in a room locked from the inside with a pistol beside the body. Perhaps it was the perfect (almost) frame. The reader will have to wait until the final paragraph to hear the old inspector's solution.

A Gathering of Killers: A Raymond Masters Mystery -

Inspector Masters is at it again - this time untangling the mystery of a murder in which the body was stabbed, shot, strangled, drowned, poisoned and bludgeoned. A dozen suspects at the beautiful Whispering Pines Lodge lead him on a merry chase as he systematically sorts away the innocent and
hones in on the culprit (or is it culprits?). Again, it remains until the final page to hear the old inspector's solution.

The Man Who Refused to Die: A Raymond Masters Mystery -

Not even the third time was to be the charm for this murderer. A beloved, retired, dying, classical guitarist is the eventual victim. In his mansion - curiously - live his three former wives, his long time back-up guitarist with his despicable son, his distant personal assistant, the charming young chauffeur with a shady past, the cook and the mysterious stranger. There is a twist at the end unlike the readers of Raymond Masters mysteries have ever before witnessed.

Revenge of the Restless Crossbow: A Raymond Masters Mystery -

Apparently of its own volition, an antique crossbow, long perched high up on the wall of the Rafferty Mansion, fires and kills one of the guests at a publisher's book launching party. The following day another member of the group is found murdered. There are a variety of suspects: three mystery writers, a universally disliked book critic, the cantankerous neighbor and his son, the wily old grounds keeper, the maid, the new assistant to Winston Rafferty (one of the writers), and a flock of pigeons. Nothing is simple this time out. The twists and turns tangle among themselves. Masters identifies the perpetrator, of course, but the reader will have to wait until the final word of the final paragraph to hear his/her name.

The Case of the Gypsy Curse: A Raymond Masters Mystery –

Seven of the past nine leaders of an off-beat fraternal order in a small Wyoming town died mysterious deaths. There have been no wounds and no traces of poison. There has, however, been a long-standing Gypsy curse against the group. Natural causes? Coincidence? Curse? Masters doesn't think so. Not only, does he nail the perpetrator(s?) of these seven crimes, but he puts the screws to four more along the way.

The Case of the Clairvoyant Kid: A Raymond Masters Mystery

At age 15 handsome, Hans Hanzik – a Bosnian orphan – is the most successful touring psychic in the U.S. A series of threats against his life brings Detective Masters into the case. Masters immediately senses trouble (the boy's guardian) and conj ours up a spell or two of his own. Though set in the Ozark Mountains, Masters manages to solve 3 outstanding homicides form NYC and Key West, while tutoring the shy, sheltered young clairvoyant in the gentle art of romance. In a spine tingling finish, Masters saves the boy and zaps the bad guys.

The Case of the Cryptogram Murders: A Raymond Masters Mystery –

Adam Williams, wealthy furrier and despicable human being, is killed while Detective Masters and the half dozen possible suspects from family and staff are with him in his study - each the perfect alibi for the others. Motives and gadgetry abound. Along the way four other murders are solved as Masters enlists the help of a fascinating group of characters - all of them suspects.

The Murders at Terrapin Island: A Raymond Masters Mystery-

The late July vacation, which Raymond Masters had been looking forward to at the *Terrapin Island* resort in Lake Huron, immediately turns to work as staff members, one after another, are murdered. Could it be the troubled teenage boy, the greedy millionaire or his pants chasing wife, the impatient artist, or the beautiful young writer who claims she is searching for her birth mother? Other suspects abound as Masters sorts through the clues with the reader.

The Butler Did It! A Raymond Masters Mystery -

Detective Raymond Masters arrives at *Windstone Manor* - high atop a tiny, remote, snow blown, island off the Maine Coast - to supervise a Scavenger Hunt designed by Elliott Stone, the aging, despicable, Lord of the Manor, to allow one of his heirs to enhance his or her position in his will. The participants include the five butlers who formerly worked for him (most of whom hate each other and Elliott), his brother and sister (who harbor long standing grudges against him), and his nephew (a self-centered, amoral, 30 year old who has lived most of his life at Windstone). Then there is Carl, his lawyer; Bea, his nurse and secretary; Angie, the cook and maid; and Hyde, the current young butler. Five bodies later, Masters (once again surviving a strange little policeman sidekick) solves the cases amid the unrelenting, freezing storm that holds the group captive on the island.

The Case of the Despicable Duo Murders: A Raymond Masters Mystery

No one shed a tear when either of them (a wealthy father and his adult son) were murdered but when one of Raymond Masters' friends is accused of doing them in, the old detective packs his bags and arrives to direct the investigation. In this twelfth book in the series, legitimately motivated suspects abound, including the maid, long mistreated by both men; the handyman, a loner and newcomer to the area; the brother, an expert marksman who had a life long feud with the family; the security guard, with unspoken motives; the drifter, whose presence seems oddly out of place; the brilliant teenage twins next door, with tempers and revenge on their minds; and their mother, recently done wrong by the son. The shot had clearly come from his friend's bedroom window yet Masters works to prove otherwise.

The Case of Too Many Suspects: A Raymond Masters Mystery

A rich, old, unlikable man is murdered by a revolver loaded with blanks. Five family members and employs confess to the crime. Each has compelling special knowledge of the crime scene. The story takes place in the Nevada desert during the week of July 4th. Masters is assisted by a pair of teenage boys. The cast of characters is colorful. The old detective manages to solve a few outstanding cases along the way.

Ozark Ghost Stories by *Marc Miller, Ghost writer*

The Specters of Carlton County

To this day the ghosts of six, teenage, confederate soldiers - *The Cowards' Patrol* - roam the Ozark backwoods, forced by an evil cleric to continue taking the war to blue clad Yankees who dare trespass into the dark summer nights of isolated, Carlton County. When a young writer, Marc Miller, travels to the area to write their story, he finds he is unwelcome both as a writer and an outsider. He hears their mournful cries at night and sees their ghostly images in the windows and mirrors of the old Inn. He encounters them on horseback, swords at the ready, galloping together across a foggy, moonlit, Civil War graveyard. Are they apparitions searching for their final peace, or are they something more sinister? Miller is a skeptic but will that continue once he meets *The Specters of Carlton County*? **ISBN: 1-885631-83-9**

The Malevolent Ghost of Charlie Chance

The Ozark Hills Academy - a rustic boarding school - sits atop a beautiful hill in the back country of Northwest Arkansas, and serves the region's disadvantaged, 13 to 19 year old boys. The area had once been owned by the long dead, Charlie Chance - known hater of children and progress. During each *Devil's Darkness* - the convergence of the dark of the moon and a strong, warm, southerly breeze - the Ghost of old Charlie selects a student and sucks his soul from his being, leaving him dead and bereft of an afterlife. Author, Marc Miller, hoping to write Charlie's story, arrives to investigate. The Ghost appears and raises havoc in an apparent attempt to get the writer to leave. It becomes a 'good ghost' - 'bad ghost' quandary for Marc and the young people who offer help. **ISBN: 1-885631-84-7**

The Kettles and the Keeps: Ghosts at War – An Ozark Mt. Ghost Story

Ghost Writer, Marc Miller, arrives in *Sandy Valley*, an isolated area of northwest Arkansas, to mediate a dispute between warring clans of ghosts - the Kettles and the Keeps who, in their mortal forms, have been feuding for more than a century. A pair of pre-Civil War Apparitions appears - one Kettle and one Keep - and unexplainably begins inflicting serious physical maladies on a dozen teenagers. The dispute escalates, once again turning the families against each other. Marc enlists the help of Willy, a teenager suddenly confined to a wheelchair and Jake, a ten year old, wise beyond his years. ISBN: 1-885631-85-5

The Haunting of Hickory Hollow

The tiny, backwoods, town of Hickory Hollow is haunted. It has been since before the Civil War. That is just they way its residents want it. They have configured a mini-theme park around the ghostly goings on and seem to have established an amicable relationship with them. Marc Miller is brought into town when mysterious accidents - some resulting in the death of local residents - begin taking place. Is it the ghostly revenge predicted by the lore? Is it the more a worldly activity related to a business takeover? There are teenage ghosts swinging from ropes, bands of galloping ghostly desperados, and suspicious strangers. And then there is the secret *Covenant* sworn to by the locals residents. Hmmm! ISBN: 1-885631-87-1

BOOKS IN THE
LITTLE PEOPLE OF THE OZARK MOUNTAINS SERIES
by Gary Hutchison

Book One: The Ring of The Farjumpers

Jay, a nine and a half year old mortal boy, and Twiggs, a twelve and three quarters year old Little Person, encounter each other for the first time. A wonderful friendship develops, which, along the way necessitates close scrutiny of the two cultures by the youngsters. Then, the relationship must end, and the boys struggle to deal with the impending loss. Humorous, nostalgic, philosophical, delightful, and thought provoking. You may just see yourself on every page. ISBN: 1-885631-94-4

Book Two: A Man of the Clan

The odyssey continues as it describes the struggles and the successes of Twiggs (the Little Person) during the first months of coping with his new responsibilities as a Man of the Clan Dewgoodabee. He finds himself in love - another set of struggles and delights. The story reminds us that growing up, though complex, need not be an unpleasant experience. A sentimental reverie of how it was and how it could be. ISBN: 1-885631-97-9

Book Three: The Ambassador and The Touchperson

Jay and Twiggs have their first three meetings. Hard-nosed negotiating doesn't interfere with joy-filled escapades at the swimming hole and cabin. The year culminates with "the miracle of the millennium," as Jay's Grampa characterizes it in his country newspaper. The boys learn that even a miracle, like life itself, sometimes has an unanticipated down-side which they struggle to understand and manage. ISBN: 1-885631-95-2

Book Four: Twiggs and Cinnamon
Twiggs and Cinnamon are wed and deal with the usual delights and adjustments that confront all young couples. A host of new Little People are introduced as they go about caring for themselves and the Mortals in the nearby hills and valleys. Hardy portions of delightful celebrations are enjoyed and an impending catastrophe is encountered. ISBN: 1-885631-94-4

Other Books by this author
(various pennames)

Crossroads (adults) ISBN: 1-885631-55-3
Gary Hutchison

A Crisis of Myths (adults) ISBN: 1-885631-16-2
Gary Hutchison

Family Portrait (adults/high school) ISBN: 1-885631-36-7
Bonnie Brewster

Everything I needed to know about saving the world I learned before I was ten (adults) ISBN: 1-885631-56-1
Craigy Franklin

The Secrets of Deep Mind Mastery (adults) ISBN: 1-885631-51-0
G. F. Hutchison

One Rule Plan for Family Happiness ISBN: 1-885631-03-0
G.F. Hutchison

Trouble-Proofing Kids ISBN: 1-885631-17-0
G. F. Hutchison

The Chipper of Oakton Villa (youth) ISBN: 1-885631-48-0
Gary Hutchison

Replacement Kid (adult/youth) ISBN: 1-885631-71-5
David Drake

Kidd's Grand Adventure (youth) ISBN: 1-885631-71-5
David Drake

The TOMMY POWERS superhero series (youth 10 -15)
David Drake
      Book 1 Sage ... ISBN: 1-885631-89-8
      Book 2 Mutant ISBN: 1-885631-45-6
      Book 3 Sorcerer ISBN: 1-885631-92-8
      Book 4 Replicator ISBN: 1-885631-83-6

Zephyr in Pinstripes (Adult/youth) ISBN: 1-885631-41-3
Craig Franklin

In Praise of the Commonplace (Seniors) ISBN: 1-885631-83-9
Grampa Gray

In Praise of Simple Pleasures (Seniors) ISBN: 1-885631-77-4
Grampa Gray

Enjoy other
FAMILY FRIENDLY
books
from

THE FAMILY OF MAN PRESS

At
www.TheHappinessPlace.com
www.familypress.com

Mysteries, Ozark Ghost Stories, Romance, Children and Teen, Senior Citizens, More.

Also
The kids – 9 to 14 – will want to take a look at

www.tommypowers.net

for FREE POSTERS and info about
Tommy Powers the 13 year, non-violent, old Super Hero.

Printed in the United States
85864LV00001B/91-144/A